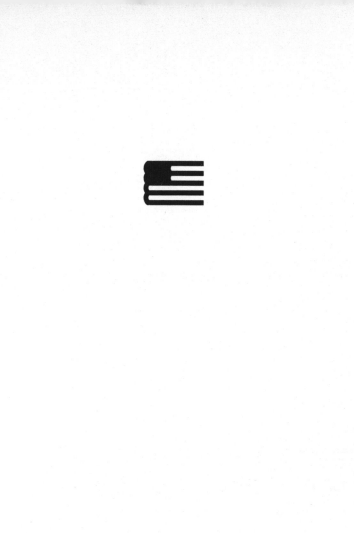

ALSO BY LAURA INGRAHAM

The Obama Diaries

Power to the People

Shut Up & Sing

The Hillary Trap

LAURA INGRAHAM

WITH RAYMOND ARROYO

Of Thee I Zing

America's Cultural Decline
from Muffin Tops to Body Shots

THRESHOLD EDITIONS

NEW YORK   LONDON   TORONTO   SYDNEY

Threshold Editions
A Division of Simon & Schuster, Inc.
1230 Avenue of the Americas
New York, NY 10020

First Threshold Editions hardcover edition July 2011

THRESHOLD EDITIONS and colophon are
trademarks of Simon & Schuster, Inc.

For information about special discounts for bulk purchases,
please contact Simon & Schuster Special Sales at
1-866-506-1949 or business@simonandschuster.com.

The Simon & Schuster Speakers Bureau can bring authors
to your live event. For more information or to book an
event contact the Simon & Schuster Speakers Bureau at
1-866-248-3049 or visit our website at www.simonspeakers.com.

Designed by Ruth Lee-Mui

Manufactured in the United States of America

1   3   5   7   9   10   8   6   4   2

ISBN 978-1-4516-4204-9
ISBN 978-1-4516-4206-3 (ebook)

Photo Credits: image from iStock: page 1; images from Getty: pages 12, 15,
20, 30, 52, 54, 58, 60, 63, 83, 115, 117, 128, 140, 160, 163, 182, 200,
221, 240, 250, 258, 262, 272, 278, 294, 295; images courtesy of the author:
pages 25, 62, 65, 66, 98, 105, 106, 109, 121, 170, 211, 234, 236, 298, 302

To Pat & Becky Cipollone, for always being there

Contents

Introduction

Give me your slackers, your bored,
Your muffin-topped masses, yearning to eat free,
The wretched refuse of your tweeting horde,
Send these, the mannerless, TMZ-tossed celebrities to me,
I lift the golden lid of my rubbish bin's door.
—The Inscription on the Statue of Liberty
  (circa 2011)

If you want to see evidence of America's cratering culture, just stop by your local shopping mall.

I had never experienced vertigo before. But as I was riding down an escalator last September at a Northern Virginia shopping mall, I became so dizzy I almost careened over the railing. It had been a while since I had braved the mall scene alone. Rushing toward me were some of the most horrifying, unsettling images I had seen since Rosie O'Donnell posted her 9/11 video blog.

Below me, on the left, was a group of six young girls wearing jeans so tight, Jacques Cousteau could have worn them on his last undersea expedition. And if he were alive today, he'd be shocked to know that humpback whales can not only survive on land, but text, snap gum, and suck down thirty-two-ounce milk shakes masquerading as coffee drinks. Then to my right, two adolescents were leaning up against a store window, shaking back their floppy bangs and fiddling with the waistbands of their jeans. Upon closer inspection, I saw they were pulling their pants down, not up, so as to showcase their pastel-colored boxer shorts. They paused briefly from their hair/underwear routine to venerate the cleavage of a model in the Victoria's Secret window display. Whatever Vicki's secret was, it appeared to be a secret no more.

As I stepped off the bottom of the escalator, I almost walked into an ugly collision. A Rascal scooter had a head-on with an over-under Bugaboo stroller. Upon impact, the elderly scootee was thrown to the ground. The infants, outfitted in Dolce & Gabbana baby couture, started wailing. In a white rage, their demure and compassionate mother cursed out Grandpa at the top of her lungs. "Do you know how much this stroller costs, old man?" she shrieked, pointing at the cracked front wheel. "More than your last Social Security check, I can tell you that!" As the dazed senior citizen struggled to get up, a forty-something guy wearing earbuds and a *Quadrophenia* T-shirt stepped right over him. The old gent just moaned.

Meanwhile, the Rascal had a mind of its own and kept rolling toward a portable kiosk where a man was getting his eyebrows threaded. The threader was so startled at the sight of the approaching scooter that she caught the tip of the man's nose in the threads. "I knew I should have gone to Elizabeth Arden!" the now bleeding thirtyish man screamed, as he jumped up.

Everywhere I turned was a fresh horror. Outside a nearby toy store, a child was splayed out on the filthy floor, kicking his mother and wailing "ZhuZhu pet! Gimme a ZhuZhu pet!" Despite her leg injuries, the mother blithely continued walking, ignoring the display. On the other side of the mall, near the food court, a family devoured individual troughs of lo mein like hyenas hollowing a carcass on the savannah. Their faces literally pressed into the bowls, not a one of them even glanced up as I brushed their table.

Overwhelmed by the visuals, I fled into a nearby coffee shop. I took a seat between a senior citizen playing FarmVille on his iPad and two teens texting in trances. They didn't even look up. Sipping my "skinny" latte, I suddenly thought, "I hate foam. I distinctly told the barista no foam." Tossing the cup aside, I stared in disbelief at the tragic panorama on all sides.

"Is this it?" I wondered. "Is this what our forefathers fought for? What my parents struggled for? Is this the American culture the Greatest Generation had in mind when they stormed the beaches at Normandy? So we could aspire to be like the Kardashians or land a role on *The Housewives of Miami*?

Our manners are shot. We dress like homeless prostitutes and derelict drug addicts. We spend countless hours social networking and end up becoming less social. Our pop culture has popped.

In areas as broad as personal grooming, recreation, education, parenting, faith, and even the way we travel, the verdict is in: we have fallen faster than a discount facelift. We're going to hell in a handbasket (and the handbasket was made in China). Even if our economic and national security challenges disapperared overnight, we'd still have to climb out of the cultural abyss into which we've tumbled.

Look around you. Do you even recognize what passes for American "culture" these days? If Thomas Jefferson were penning a Declaration of Independence for America today, he might write:

"When in a coarse state of human events, it becomes necessary for one people to dissolve the bonds between themselves and the cultural blight degrading the Republic ... they should declare the causes which impel them to separation ..."

What follows are "the causes" that compel us to sever ties with this culture, halt its decline, and find a better way. It is a patriotic intervention. When you love something you fight for it—and I can't bear to see America go down like this.

The first step toward recovery is admitting we have a problem. Since others are either incapable or too distracted to identify the cultural threats afflicting America, I take the patriotic duty upon myself. Herein I will point out the cell phone barkers; the four telltale signs you are in a lousy restaurant; our penchant for inane exercise fads; the worst children's names in American history; our idiotic fixation with high-end cupcakes; each fraudulent holiday created by the card industry; and the young people who, like, speak in grunts, not full sentences.

So bring along your gas mask and something to protect yourself—we're going deep into the nether regions of American culture. As harrowing as this journey may be, it is also rife with hilarity. So rejoice, fellow Americans! Our cultural renewal begins here.

I

"Mommy, Make It Stop!"

Parenting is hard work, as any mom or dad will attest. Just when you think you have children figured out, they grow and change on you. But there are a number of things that parents do (or refuse to do) along the way that can throw a monkey wrench into the situation. It doesn't take a PhD in early childhood education to understand that horrible behavior and crude actions of the child can be directly traced back to the parents. Usually, the more knowledgeable a mother or father is about parenting "trends," and the more parenting magazines they subscribe to, the more screwed up the kid. These parents make "old-school" moms and dads feel guilty. They spend hours making fresh, hormone-free baby food in the blender, surfing the Net for *Your Baby Can Read* DVDs, and ferrying their toddlers around to Mandarin and Arabic classes.

Children are being robbed of their childhood by those who are supposed to love them most. Kids' lives are over-scheduled and insanely stressful. They've barely learned their ABC's before they're diagnosed with ADD. Parents' "more is more" approach often starts well before baby is born and follows the child through college and beyond.

Maternity 9-1-1

My mother had me when she was in her forties. She smoked and drank socially for the entire pregnancy. The extent of her preparation for the birth of her first child (my brother Jimmy) was packing a bag to take to the hospital. Back then, having children was just what you did, not something requiring a "birth plan" and endless strategy sessions. Today, women who have a laid-back attitude about pregnancy are cultural misfits, shunned by the parenting-industrial complex. "Maternity consultants" are all the rage. They instruct ladies about a range of "pre-conception, pregnancy, post-partum and parenting topics." I can almost hear my mother now: "You mean you pay someone to tell you that childbirth hurts, and that you have to push the baby out? Honey, women are born to do that. It would be like paying someone to tell us how to flirt." (She'd be shocked to learn that now women pay for that advice, too!) Bravo cable network has tapped into this sad phenomenon with the show *Pregnant in Heels*, hosted by "maternity concierge" Rosie Pope. She helps rich women turn their baby's gestation period into one nine-month-long trip to the spa at Canyon Ranch. A self-described "pregnancy guru," Pope assists expectant moms with their pressing, critical dilemmas, such as arranging for the perfect stylist to do pre-birth hair and makeup. Gotta look fab for the ultimate delivery room close-up! Heaven forbid, the first thing your baby sees is your chipped nail polish and unwaxed bikini line! At this rate, it's only a matter of time before the umbilical cord gets its own lighting consultant!

"Expert"-Proofing Your Children

My mother bottle-fed all of us. We also ate Beech-Nut Baby Food and grapes that weren't cut up into eighths. When we started crawling she kept stuff like bleach and Windex under the kitchen sink—not under lock and key. She had a wooden playpen where she stuck us when she had to vacuum. Today my mother would be considered a danger to herself and her children. A nosy neighbor might even contemplate reporting her to the authorities.

Long before a mother feels her first contraction, she feels the real pressure. The push comes from "baby" businesses marketing products and services that neither we nor our babies need. Moms who should just be enjoying their pregnancies become needlessly panicked and paranoid. Pass the Pampers. I was on the cusp of becoming that woman when I was convinced by a friend to hire a "baby-proofing" technician to safeguard my thirteen-month-old son from the perils of toilet bowls, sharp table corners, and fireplace implements. Two officious-looking "home safety analysts" with clipboards spent an hour studying every inch of my home and documenting the hazards that awaited my toddler. The estimate for addressing the dangers was fifteen pages long, and included: "swivel latches" on my television to help prevent tipping, fireplace screen anchors, furniture straps for every dresser, and elasticized foam padding for all coffee and end tables (just for starters). They lost me on page 4, so I skipped to the last page. The total for all this peace of mind: $2,996.91. (As if by keeping it under 3K, I would think I was getting a bargain.) When I asked a neighbor mom whether this quote was in the ballpark, she responded earnestly: "You can't put a price on your child's safety." No, but apparently you can put a price on gullibility. I discovered she had paid almost double the amount for the same "safe start baby-proofing" of her home.

Determined to fight back in my own way against this insanity, I headed to the hardware store, bought some basic safety gates, outlet covers and plastic cabinet latches and installed them myself. The cost was about two hundred dollars. Oh, and of course, I immediately went out and bought a playpen. People called it my baby jail. I called it nirvana. In fact, the trouble began when I gave my son his "get out of jail free" card. The little bugger locked himself in three different bathrooms—including one in a friend's house in Florida. But just think of all the drama he would have been deprived of, had we slapped those $1.99 plastic guards on the doorknobs!

Stupid Kid Names

Children should not be named after a piece of furniture, a planet, a fruit, or an herb. Today's little ones are saddled with some of the most ridiculous names ever—it's as if the parents are trying to force the kids to hate them early.

There are consequences for the name you confer on your child. According to a 2009 study in *Social Science Quarterly*, a child's first name can predispose him to a life of crime and incarceration. The top ten most dangerous names for boys are: Alec, Ernest, Garland, Ivan, Kareem, Luke, Malcolm, Preston, Tyrell, and Walter. The odder the name, the more ridicule the boy is likely to encounter in life. Reporter Erin Burnett explained it this way on the *Today* show: "Basically, if you're teased mercilessly your entire childhood for your name, you become an angry, bitter person, and you lash out in a way that could be negative." Certainly there are exceptions to the rule (but Alec Baldwin isn't one of them).

Celebrities have escalated the baby name stupidity, tempting the public to ruin their children's lives as well. The Naked Chef, Jamie Oliver, and his wife Jools (another winner of a name), are raising what sounds like a victory garden at home. Their daughters are named—and I am not joking—Daisy Boo, Poppy Honey Rosie, and Petal Blossom Rainbow. But these celebri-tot names can't be topped:

- Apple and Moses (Gwyneth Paltrow). I think she's going for an Old Testament theme here.

- Sparrow Madden (Nicole Richie). Does Sparrow tweet?
- Bronx Mowgli (Pete Wentz and Ashlee Simpson). Hope he's a Yankee fan.
- Pilot Inspektor (Jason Lee). A future FAA official?
- Denim and Deizel (Toni Braxton). I guess Wash and Wear were already taken.
- Jermajesty (Jermaine Jackson). The sibling will be called Jerhighness.
- Blanket (Michael Jackson). Why not Glove?
- Bamboo (Outkast's Big Boi). Is he trying to ensure his son's also an outcast?
- Kyd (David Duchovny and Tea Leoni). You're kydding me.
- Mars, Puma, and Seven (Erykah Badu). A candy bar, a sneaker, and a lucky number. Why not go for three more? Mounds, Adidas, and Eight?

One day, these children are going to grow up and they will either legally change their names or just march into their parents' bedroom one night and beat them to a pulp. The research suggests the latter.

"We're Pregnant"

Occasionally, a male friend will come up to me at a social function and proudly announce: "We're pregnant."

"I didn't know you had a uterus, Tom," is what I feel like saying.

I realize that the husband is trying to be part of the process and indicate his solidarity with his wife, but how much weight did he gain? The First Amendment doesn't protect shouting "Fire!" in a crowded theater, and it shouldn't protect this grating social construction. "We're" not anything. Your wife is pregnant, and will soon give birth. You'll be taking the video.

There are also men who take this "we're pregnant" line to the extreme, actually exhibiting symptoms of pregnancy. Some men report having experienced morning sickness, food cravings, even labor pains. Physicians suggest that these sympathy pains are the result of hormonal irregularities and stress. And guys, if you feel an actual baby coming on, may I suggest you lay off the late-night quesadillas.

Lactating Daddies

Few would argue against the health and bonding benefits of breastfeeding your baby, but does Daddy have to get in on the act?

Recent media reports have revealed a fact that I don't think any of us needed to know: men can and do lactate. (This must be a subset of the men described in the previous section.) ABC News reports that "a man simply being overweight could ... set the stage for lactating." The excess fat can increase estrogen levels in the body and bring on milk production. Well, I guess this is one way for that sleep-deprived mother to get some help. "I'm really tired tonight, Bob. Can you do the overnight feeding?"

There is, in fact, a community of people (largely feminists, I think) who have become crusaders for male breastfeeding. These activists encourage men to pump their chests until milk comes in so they can feed the little ones. Silly me. I thought "milkmen nostalgia" meant something entirely different! Swedish designer Ronnie Asterberg has even created something he calls Man:MILK, a "shirt that provides easy and masculine breast-feeding for men." The pockets unbutton to allow dad to expose his inner mother. Thankfully, all the medical research I have read indicates that it is extremely rare for a man who is not taking female hormones to produce enough milk to sustain a child. And any man who would desire such a thing needs to proceed imme-diately to a monster truck rally.

That Man in the Baby Sling

The only thing possibly less masculine than men who breastfeed are men who wear baby slings! And no, I'm not convinced to the contrary by those who say, "But it's so nice to see a father nurtur-ing and protecting his baby." If a man wants to protect his baby, all he needs are arms strong enough to beat the living daylights out of anyone who threatens her. One could argue that a baby sling is, in fact, a magnet for trouble. Is a thug likely to hassle a guy with a pastel-colored cotton cradle hanging across his chest, or one with broad shoulders and sturdy biceps, holding his child the old-fashioned way?

Fellas, if you are content to look like a kangaroo who just hopped off a parade float in South Beach, you can buy "The Man Sling" at ModMum.com. Though the apparatus sounds like an athletic supporter, it is actually an "army green cotton canvas" baby sling. The Web ad features a manly-looking guy wearing the contraption while hiking. (It would have been more believable to see him "slinged-out" at an Erica Jong lecture.) The sales pitch: "[R]eal men carry their baby in comfort and style with the one and only Man Sling!" Then the hard sell: "This sling has a rugged look but is soft against the baby's skin." There's something deeply unsettling about men who give up the single life for the "slingle" life. God bless these men who are actually spending time with their children, but consider the warning from my pal P.C. from the Bronx: "Slip on one of those front-loading papoose things and your testosterone level drops fifty percent."

Political bias alert! I would bet that 99.8 percent of all men who wear baby slings are liberals.

Stretch Strollers

The "children's goods" market is roaring back from a recession-induced lull. The *Washington Post* reports that in 2010 we spent $18 billion on everything from enviro-friendly changing tables to educational toys—the perfect time for the company Bugaboo to roll out its $1,500 double stroller, called the "Donkey." (A fitting name for both the contraption and parents who buy it.) Shopping for baby and toddler "luxury items" has become an obsession for moms and dads who are more concerned with boosting their own social status than ensuring their child's comfort and safety. One must make that good first impression at the playground or in line at Starbucks. After all, nothing says upper crust like a baby mover that costs more than most folks make in a week. Today's trendiest strollers come outfitted with a drink

holder, onboard mobile, and a cell phone or iPad pocket. What's next, a rear-mounted backup camera and a built-in GPS? Soon the kids will be able to take themselves out for a stroll.

Thank goodness, "stroller envy" is an affliction I have never suffered from. (For the record: I have one stroller, given to me by my friend Pinky, after she had used it for her three kids. Made of simple orange canvas and priced originally under eighty bucks, it has rolled through so many airports, it should have its own passport.)

Ingraham rule of thumb: if your stroller needs its own parking spot or requires an emissions inspection, the thing is too large. The best are the couples who have one child, but a stroller big enough to hold Michael Moore. There is no reason for a baby stroller to be that large. Unless parents are going to strap on a bonnet and start shaking their own rattles, this is a sinful purchase.

Goodnight Moon . . . and Jasper Johns

Shortly after bringing my first child home, I realized I wasn't like most other moms in my neighborhood. They seemed so organized. They were up on the latest innovations in early child development, knew all the best soccer camps, already had their three-year-olds learning a second language. But I really noticed my shortcomings in the children's room décor department— especially the nursery. Growing up as I did in a two-bedroom house, with three older brothers, the only "nursery" I knew was the garden and plant store downtown. From their exquisitely appointed baby furniture to monogrammed designer sheets made of the finest Egyptian cotton, kids today learn from an early age that the world revolves around them. And their moms have more things to show off to the neighbors!

I admit I'm a throwback. My crib was at the foot of my parents' bed in their very tight bedroom. Somehow I survived. Today, if you don't have a separate, perfectly coordinated room for your baby, people are ready to start a telethon for you. Do we really need to bring in Larry Gagosian to consult on baby Madison's art collection while she's still in utero? Will that Rothko you landed at the Sotheby's auction really mean more to her than paint from Sherwin-Williams? A few years back, I attended a charity event at the home of a young mother who seemed perfectly sane, balancing a part-time job at a law firm while raising two young children, including a new baby boy. Then she let it slip that she had flown in an acclaimed artist to create an original "whimsical" fairytale storyboard on her newborn son's nursery wall. The scene included multicolored ducks, elaborately painted bunnies, towering willow trees, and an odd cow wearing a top hat. It cost more than I paid for my first house. For Christmas last year, they brought the same artist back to paint a new scene over this magnum opus, after their older son had drawn mustaches on all the characters with a black Sharpie pen. That boy had good taste.

In my house, I have this nutty theory that if my children are in their rooms staring at the walls, I have a problem that *Architectural Digest* can't fix.

Play Hates

I remember fondly my mother announcing the first of many playdates she had arranged for me: "Laura, go outside and play. I need to get supper started." She didn't care if I was climbing a tree, playing tag with the neighbors, or throwing rocks against the boulder in the backyard. Playtime was unstructured, unpredictable and fun. Today we need full-time assistants to keep our children's playdate schedules.

First of all, I have to confess I am an occasional playdate-arranger myself. My first adventure with this phenomenon was not a pleasant one. One of my daughter's four-year-old classmates came to our house for the afternoon. She was an adorable little girl with an impossibly cute brown bob hairstyle. When she saw the few baskets of games and dolls in the basement playroom, she blurted out, "Are these all the toys you have? Is this it?" I was tempted to respond, "No Sally, we actually have an entire toy-making factory in the backyard, but we only open that to polite, well-behaved children." Sally did not make a return visit.

There are some mothers who create elaborate and involved playdate "experiences" for the tots. Talk about overkill! Does my child really need to go on a scavenger hunt for organic veggies in an acquaintance's backyard? And as I am desperately trying to get rid of junk at my house, I will take a pass on accepting "playdate" goodie bags! My neighbor's son recently came home from a playdate with puppets made from recycled plastic bottles and pipe cleaners. What's next? Will my liberal pals give visiting children goodie bags containing Michelle and Barack Obama origami figures—with an extra "Bo" left over that can be made at home? (I can't even fold the bottom sheet on the bed and I'm supposed to teach five-year-olds an ancient Japanese art form?) Let's be clear: these are playdate swag bags! I can't take the pressure. If my children's friends leave my house with anything, it would more likely be a skinned knee or a stomachache.

When we used to play outside with our friends, time seemed lazy and limitless. It ended only when Mom called us in for dinner. But now we not only place hard limits on the kids' playtime, but everything else is dictated, too. The end result: too much structure, not enough fun. Parents pick out and oversee the crafts that kids are allowed to do, right down to the type of felt markers that are "allowed" on the table. What happened to improvisatory play that allows children to develop their creative imaginations?

Kids' playdates have become an extension of school rather than a break from it.

Let's be blunt: playdates are often just free babysitting. How many mothers will admit to dumping their kid(s) off at other people's homes while they go get their nails done? (No comment!) And how many of us arrange playdates for our children when they are really playdates for ourselves—an opportunity for the mothers to share a glass of wine and chitchat. (Guilty! I have my own personalized copy of *The Three Martini Playdate*.)

At least I make a point of trying to know the parents and their values before entrusting my son or daughter to their care. You get the sense that some of these parents have spent more time getting to know their dog walkers than the moms (and nannies) who are hosting their children's playdates. Why are we surprised when our sons start using the F-bomb in casual conversation or when our daughters start shaking their "booties" and humming Rihanna's "S&M"?

What's more dangerous—letting your son run around the yard with a bubble wand and a Nerf gun or dropping him off at the house of someone you barely know so he can spend the afternoon playing Grand Theft Auto and roaming around on Facebook in the rec room?

"It's my party and I'll cry— if I don't have a petting zoo"

Remember the good old days when a birthday party for a six-year-old involved nothing more than a homemade sheet cake, store-brand vanilla ice cream, paper hats from the drugstore, and (if you were really splurging) a cardboard pin-the-tail-on-the-donkey game? The really rich kids got to invite six friends to the McDonald's birthday party room. Those days are long gone.

I fell into this party trap a few years ago. When the Sleeping Beauty moon-bounce arrived at my house, I felt like I had done something special for my daughter. Until, that is, I overheard one of the pre-K invitees groan, "Not *another* moon-bounce!" Little did I know, I was behind the party curve. To be truly memorable, a child's party now must be an over-the-top, choreographed adventure complete with its own stylist and professional photographer.

- **Farm Parties:** Horses, sheep and assorted livestock are trucked in to entertain invited guests. The stench of these movable petting zoos is particularly unpleasant in warm weather. It used to be that pony rides were restricted to the carnival or the county fair. No more. Now they can happen right on your front lawn. To keep up with the Joneses, do we now have to bring in a big top and P. T. Barnum himself?

- **Spa Parties:** Not long ago, my five-year-old daughter came home from her friend Cynthia's birthday party looking unusually relaxed and in a great mood. I immediately noticed that her fingernails and toenails were exquisitely manicured. Hello Kitty! stared back at me from every digit. It turns out there were "mani-" and "pedi-" stations at this soirée. Each girl had her own dedicated beautician. Hand, shoulder, and foot massages were included. When girls are pouting because there are no seaweed wraps and oxygen facials—we know we have created pampered monsters. During my mother's seventy-nine years on this earth, after decades of working her tail off as a waitress and a housewife, the only spa she knew was the Tupperware basin that she soaked her feet in at the end of a long day. For her, splurging was adding the Epsom salts.

- **Laser Tag and Gym Parties:** These parties are a plaintiff attorney's dream. If you are interested in spending most of Saturday night in an emergency room, make sure your son or daughter is invited to one of these accident-prone shindigs. You feel like you've entered some twisted 1980s music video when you walk into one of these laser tag joints. It doesn't take the Supernanny to know that fog + strobe lights + cramped quarters = disaster for a dozen rambunctious boys. Inevitably, somebody gets a black eye or trampled before the buzzer goes off. The gym parties are just as bad. Cake and ice cream are preceded by kids going through Olympic-style events in rapid succession. Unless your daughter has been coached by Shannon Miller herself, the safest party games for her might not be the uneven bars and the vault.

- *Princess Parties:* Once upon a time ... a very indulgent mother contracted with a local theater's wardrobe department to help costume her daughter's birthday production. The guests were expected to choose costumes from rolling racks where princess gowns, jewelry and tiaras hung. They were then forced to mingle with college students moonlighting as fairy tale characters. Brother, was it Grimm! Little girls who thought they were coming for cake and ice cream had to sing for their supper—literally. Before they knew what was happening, the girls were cast in skits adapted from *Snow White* and *Cinderella.* Does the pressure to perform ever end?
- *Face Painting Parties:* You bring your child to a party, and she is suddenly set upon by maniacs with paintbrushes. These are people you wouldn't let paint your

house, let alone your kid's face. After one of these painting extravaganzas, I was horrified to find my poor daughter covered with brown, black, and white makeup, looking like a mangy cheetah. Was she just cast in the touring company of *Cats*? Then when I suggested washing it off, I thought she was going to call Child Protective Services. "You can't take this off, Mommy!! I'm a cheetaaaaaaah!" Nothing was really lost by removing the paint. Like the Shroud of Turin, the image is there forever on my brand-new white Turkish bath towel.

Snackers

When did breakfast, lunch and dinner fail to provide enough nourishment for our children? Snacking has now become the kids' second, fourth, and fifth meals of the day. When I was little, a snack was the piece of fruit you grabbed on the way out to play in the yard around 3 p.m. Now, to be considered a good parent, the kids need access to a replenished buffet throughout the day, as if they were on a Carnival Cruise. The list goes on and on: yogurt, pudding, applesauce, Cheerios, pretzels, cookies. And this book isn't long enough to rattle on about the gourmet fare parents lavish on their children—not to mention the scorn heaped upon those of us who offer other children uncool snacks such as grapes or saltines. "Oh, I'm sorry, Phoebe only eats gluten-free, salt-free, dairy-free crackers." No, Phoebe didn't have an allergy, but I think I'm developing one to her mom.

Juice Addicts

There are questions that continue to vex mankind. Is there a universe beyond ours? How and when did the first stars and galaxies come into being? Why is time different from other dimensions? And how did American parents ever raise productive, healthy, well-adjusted children without the "juice box"?

When I grew up, it was a big treat to have frozen grape juice (Welch's) from a can. It was a beautiful crystallized purple concentrate that my mother mixed in a glass pitcher and kept cold in the fridge. My brothers and I usually had a small glass in the mornings. We didn't drink juice all day long. Now our kids feel deprived if their lunch boxes (fancy insulated designer or themed bags) don't include a juice box or pouch. My favorites are the mini-boxes—one sip, and it's history. And admit it, you feel guilty if you don't buy into "organic" food marketing foolishness. Check out the multi-pack of Earth's Best Organic Tots Aseptic Strawberry Pear Juice, 4.23 ounce variety. I don't even know what the word "aseptic" means, but I don't like the sound of it. A favorite among the fancy mom set are juice pouches produced by a company brilliantly branded "Honest." So we are supposed to feel better about the ten grams of sugar our child is getting because the packaging reads "Honest Kids Goodness Grapeness." It is honest about this: "just one sip and you'll be hooked forever." It's never too early to teach our kids the lingo of addiction!

A Failure to Correct

How many of us have had entire movies ruined because a child sitting behind us is kicking our seat? Their parents see them doing it but do nothing.

I have read parenting manuals that instruct us to allow children to "emotionally express themselves" even by demonstrating bad behavior. They say we have to "offer children other behavior choices" while not showing displeasure. I saw a mother at a clothing store recently who was obviously a devotee of this "strategy." She permitted her son to punch her on the legs repeatedly, while screaming "I hate you" at the top of his lungs. Once she reached the checkout, she bought the kid a chocolate bar. If we, the aggrieved public, responded to this mother's behavior the same way, we'd have to buy her a Mercedes.

The placid nature of some parents in the face of horrendous

behavior astounds me. One time at a baseball game, a boy of about twelve started tossing peanuts at people seated in the deck below. The spectators being pelted by the nuts started to complain. What did the father do? He pretended he didn't hear them and bought the kid a team shirt between innings.

Time-Out for Time-Outs

It is unbelievable to me that some parents still think "time-outs" are effective. This parenting "strategy" became the sensible, mature parent's answer to spanking, which we've been told is mean, cruel, and counterproductive. So, if little Lance is pulling the family dog's ear, Mommy sends him to the stairs to sit for a few minutes. Oh great, the dog has already suffered, so the carpeting on the stairs should as well? Why do we think children who poke the pet or push their siblings are going to be any nicer to their time-out spot in the house? I have seen banisters scratched, rug fibers pulled, and walls written on during time-outs. My mother never sent me to the "corner" when I misbehaved. She was smart enough to know I would probably cause more mayhem there than I did at the table.

If we are brutally honest with one another, we'll admit that time-outs are more for the beleaguered parent who needs a time-out from the stress of it all. If Joey goes to his time-out, Mommy can finish her phone call or vegetable chopping for that night's dinner. The "time-outers" are usually the same ones who grimace at the mere mention of spanking. For certain liberal elites, there is one continuum from swatting children on the fanny to water-boarding innocent locals. One of the best and most involved fathers I know says it best—if you spank once, you may never have to do it again. The parents who should be reported to Child Protective Services aren't the occasional bottom whackers, but the ones who indulge their kids with the latest behavioral adjustment fad.

The Disaster in Aisle 5

If your child is defiling a public space, it is probably a good idea to remove said child from the premises immediately. For some inexplicable reason, I have encountered parent after parent who allow their children to do inexcusable things without any concern for those around them.

Case in point: I am walking down the aisle of a big-box store when a little girl begins to projectile vomit in all directions. (I nearly threw up myself.) The mother is standing there placidly sipping her Frappuccino, watching the child retch as if this were the fountain show at the Bellagio. "That popcorn mustn't have agreed with your tummy," the mother says calmly. Since the entire contents of the child's stomach are covering the aisle, this seems obvious. After the poor girl has nothing else to bring up, the mother pulls out a wet wipe, runs it over the kid's mouth, and escorts Linda Blair out as if nothing had happened. She doesn't alert management, she doesn't try to clean up the toxic pond in aisle 5—she just walks out.

Another time I was at a toy store in the stuffed animal section, when a woman arrived pushing a shopping cart with her toddler on board. He had huge blue saucer eyes and an impish grin. How sweet, I thought. Sweet, that is, until I saw him flicking the contents of his diaper all over the teddy bears on the shelf next to him. The pink bears were suddenly speckled brown. In disgust, I turned away, imagining I would soon hear an outraged reaction from his mother. Several seconds went by. Not a sound. When I turned around, the mother was moving the dung-covered teddies to the back of the shelf. She then wheeled her little Jackson Pollack away to wreak havoc on another part of the store. Imagine her reaction if a fellow shopper's child had spread his diaper waste all over her $5,000 yellow Birkin Bag. (Yes, I imagined it.)

The Designer Kid

There is always at least one fashion plate in every group of kids— that child who looks as if she just stepped out of Anna Wintour's closet. The little darling has perfectly coordinated clothes, a matching houndstooth hat and scarf, and a pair of soft leather riding boots. If like Zeus, Ralph Lauren could give birth to fully clad offspring from his forehead—it would look like this.

Children's bodies grow at such alarming rates, why would anyone spend several thousand dollars on clothes that they might wear twice if they're lucky? Last summer I saw a precocious little girl wearing someone else's name on every part of her body. She had a $200 Armani top, $140 Ugg boots, and $98 Patch Flare Jeans from Juicy Couture. (What, no Cartier tank watch?) But heck, I'm into luxury clothes for my kids, too. Perhaps you've heard of this Parisian outfitter? T.J.Maxx.

Like Daughter, Like Mommy

You've seen these moms. They are undeniably middle-aged (like me) but think that by squeezing into their daughters' skintight, low-cut Versace T-shirt, none of us is going to notice. I often wonder how much time must be required to maintain their hair and eyelash extensions, lip and face plumping, and constant wardrobe updating.

There's even a commercial for Tide "Acti-Lift" with a story line featuring a mom who hits a dance club wearing her daughter's green satin blouse. Those "I-Can-Still-Wear-That" moms are often quite attractive underneath it all, but they may be damaging more than their daughter's size 4 cashmere tank top. In her book *Will I Ever Be Good Enough? Healing the Daughters of Narcissistic Mothers,* author Karyl McBride claims that 1.5 million women suffer from Narcissistic Personality Disorder, and many of them compare their looks and body size to those of their daughters. The result: the daughter grows up with depleted self-esteem and low self-confidence—but at least mom enjoyed hearing those wolf whistles at the mall.

London's *Daily Mail* recently covered the tragic case of fifty-year-old Janet Cunliffe, a mother who spent tens of thousands of dollars cosmetically altering her appearance to match that of her twenty-two-year-old daughter. "Who wouldn't want to look like her?" Cunliffe told the reporter. "The way I see it is that she got her looks from me in the first place—mine have just faded with age." You'll be happy to know that Mommy and her clone regularly hit the clubs together, where strangers mistake them for trampy sisters.

Mother dearest, your attempt at a comeback ain't pretty. Stop trying to be Cher. No one is paying two hundred bucks to see you in Vegas, and you can't turn back time.

"*Prostitots* "

The mothers described above are often also guilty of the fashion crimes of their daughters. Preteens and teens are now wearing clothing that increasingly makes them look like future employees at the Mustang Ranch. Streetwalker chic has replaced cute and age-appropriate tops and skirts. These parents who allow their daughters to leave the house wearing glued-on low-rider jeans and belly-baring spaghetti strap tanks are often the same people with the "Keep Your Theology off My Biology" stickers on their Volvos. This isn't "grrrl power"—this is just gross.

If you complain about any of this, highbrow people will respond thusly: "Oh, don't be a fuddy-duddy, every generation thinks the next generation is going to the dogs." Well, in this case, the doghouse is filled with thongs, push-up bras for seven-year-olds, thigh-strangling jeans, fishnet stockings, platform stilettos, and slinky shirts bearing the subtle message "High Beams On."

We have reached a new low in our already hypersexualized culture. There are now "anti-aging" cosmetic lines for the tween set. And among the "must-have" products sold under brands such as "geoGirl" are exfoliators, mascara, and blush. This consumer class reportedly has $2 billion in buying power, which means parents are shelling out the cash to teach their young daughters that beauty really is skin deep. I have an idea: since these parents want their kids to dress and look like adults, let's complete the role reversal and put *them* in diapers and *Toy Story* pajamas with footies!

2

Missed Manners

Manners are the leading indicators of a culture. If the manners of a society have gone to pot, so has the society. Manners reveal what we think of ourselves, how we value others, and whether or not we were raised by a pack of wolves. Somewhere along the line, speaking and acting in a way that would make our parents (or grandparents) proud became a sign of submission, of mindless conformity. Things began to go downhill with the countercultural revolution of the 1960s, when a new generation decided to rebel against what it viewed as the constricting, conservative mores of the World War II generation. Since then, with each passing year, our way of speaking, behaving, and treating others has declined. Many were led to believe that manners: (a) are for losers (uncool) and (b) inhibit individuality. There's also the (c) group—those who reply, "Manners? I have no idea what you're talking about." Psychologists also downplay the idea that bad behavior, crude language, and slovenly dress are signs of deeper cultural wounds. Sociologists point out that this conduct once frowned upon is merely part of the evolutionary process, a way for individuals to create their own unique personas.

My answer to this psychobabble: if this is evolution, we're evolving in the wrong direction. It's time to clean up our collective act before we start picking bugs off each other's arm hair. It's time to call out the uncouth, the ill-mannered, and those who perpetuate this behavior through political correctness and willful ignorance. Perhaps I should boil it down to terms the ungrammatical among us can understand: "Manner up!"

Teach Your Children (and Yourselves) How to, Like, Speak

If you're like me, you're surprised when a young person actually looks you in the eye and with proper diction, answers your question or responds to your greeting. You're flabbergasted when you hear not grunts, muttering, or "uh-huhs," but strange words such as "yes" or "no," "thank you" or "please." The Horse Whisperer gets more meaningful responses from the equine set than I get from the youth I attempt to engage in conversation.

On the rare chance that your young conversant does attempt to speak to you using subjects, verbs, and an occasional direct object, you will also likely hear three other words with great frequency: "like" (or the variant "it's like") and "you know." This conversational padding is used to stall while they think of something to say. It's a crutch for the verbally lame, a bad verbal habit that began with adolescents but now has infected adults as well. Try this little experiment: ask everyone you know under the age of thirty to describe a sunset. I promise, you'll get answers such as: "You know, it's beautiful. It's, like, really wide and bright and, like, colors the whole sky." No, I don't know—or I wouldn't be asking you. And it isn't "like" really wide. It is simply "really wide." By the time these people finish adding all their superfluous syntax and annoying asides, we have lost the thread and are ready to, like, stop speaking with them, like, forever, you know?

Curse You, Potty Mouth

"What the f#*k, dude?" shouted the twentyish college student at his friend, as they were getting out of their Jeep in front of the liquor store next to my dry cleaners. "Screw you, d#*kwad! I didn't take your f#*king keys!" They both looked right at me and my two children as we walked by and didn't seem a bit embarrassed. In fact, they kept shouting at each other. My five-year-old daughter looked at me with her big brown innocent eyes and asked, "Mommy, what kind of a name is 'd#*kwad'?" After an awkward pause, I said, "Those boys are not behaving nicely, and we should pray for them." (Privately, I thought—what a waste of college tuition.)

Our culture is producing "men" who think it is entirely acceptable to swear in front of women and children. There was a time when men confined their off-color talk to bars and locker rooms. No more. They now feel free to curse with abandon in public. Women have also gotten into the act, and they can regularly be heard cursing on cell phones and at their friends and boyfriends in public. When someone who is offended says (as I often do), "Hey, please watch your mouth!" they invariably respond with something like "Shut up, b#tch!"

Obviously, kids pick up and repeat what they hear. *Time* reported (September 22, 2010) that children today are swearing at younger ages than ever before. British linguistics researcher Timothy Jay noted, "By the time kids go to school now, they're saying all the words that we try to protect them from . . . swearing really takes off between [ages] three and four." I remember the first real profanity I ever used in front of my mother. I was twelve years old and the word was "sucked." My mother's reaction was so immediate and severe that to this day, I wince when I hear (and utter!) the word. I can't imagine what she'd say about how low we've sunk today.

Of course, Hollywood has only made things worse by producing music, films, and television shows rife with gratuitously nasty language that our kids soak in and then spit back in their own conversations. The Parents Television Council released a study in November 2010 showing that there had been an almost 70 percent jump in bad language on broadcast television over the last five years. Words like "ass," "crap," and "hell" are now commonplace, along with many other slurs for parts of the male and female anatomy. It's just not that big of a deal to the entertainment set. And they can usually get away with stuff the rest of us never would (or should). Have you ever heard Margaret Cho or Kathy Griffin do stand-up? They might be the funniest women since Lucille Ball and Lily Tomlin, but it's hard to tell through their sewer mouths. (Could they get through a forty-minute set without dropping the F-bomb? If so, would they just bomb?) I find this style of "comedy" lazy and crude. It dumbs down a culture that cannot afford to lose another brain cell.

Shouldn't we care more about how this trickles down to our kids? One prominent Hollywood player clearly does not. Former *90210* actress Tori Spelling lit up the celeblogosphere a while back when she crowed that she intended to continue her own foul-mouth musings after her kids were born. Her explanation: "I'm kind of a little girl potty mouth because I say it with such vulnerability. I don't have to censor myself in front of my son, it's not that bad." And who can forget the Christian Bale profanity-laced rant on the set of the film *Terminator Salvation*? It was all over YouTube a few years ago, and spawned legions of online satirical spoofs. (I admit that if I was forced to act in that tired old film series, I might say things on set that I regretted, too.)

Words in Need of Revival

The same people who are unfazed when profanity is spewed out in public are usually the first to claim offense when perfectly reasonable descriptors are used in everyday conversation. Some of these words are historically important and not interchangeable with their politically correct variants. They have gotten a bad rap, and I am hereby launching my own campaign to bring them back. Political correctness be damned—wait, I'm not supposed to say that.

- *Hooligan:* A violent youth; just about any rapper.
- *Bum:* If you are standing on a street corner wearing a bathrobe, clutching a bottle of malt liquor, and having a heated argument with yourself—you're not homeless, you're a bum. (You might also be George Michael.)
- *Hobo:* A bum in motion, especially pushing a stolen shopping cart.
- *Strumpet:* A promiscuous woman (e.g., Paris Hilton).
- *Harlot:* See above.
- *Doxy:* See above.
- *Jezebel:* The wife of Ahab, King of Israel in the Old Testament; any shameless and immoral woman. See above.
- *Harpy:* A scolding, nagging, bad-tempered woman. (Note: I am not thinking of Joy Behar.)
- *Galoot:* A clumsy oaf. (As in, "Ed Schultz is a big galoot.")
- *Palooka:* A stupid, uncouth person.
- *Poltroon:* A coward (e.g., John "My Little Pony" Edwards).

- *Degenerate:* A person who is immoral, corrupt (e.g., Hugh Hefner).
- *Dirty Old Man:* See above, add Larry King.
- *Scoundrel:* A dishonest person (e.g., Bill Clinton).
- *Cad:* See above.
- *Wastrel:* A wasteful person; spendthrift; alt. an idler or good-for-nothing (e.g., Barack Obama).
- *Urchin:* A poorly dressed, malnourished child (e.g., the Olsen twins).

First-Namers

Don't you detest it when people keep repeating your first name in a single conversation? You come across them at cocktail parties or at business meetings when someone is trying to convince you to do something—as if the repetition of your first name will somehow lull you into a trance, making you do whatever they desire. I have yet to be persuaded. It's usually a tactic employed by people who want to sell you junk you don't need. You've heard them before: "Laura, this is an opportunity like no other. I'm telling you, Laura, once you sign on to this program, Laura, all your problems are over. Honestly, Laura, this is the way for you to go, Laura." Most of these people have read too many *Getting to Yes*–type books. They are also often the same people who use the phrase "to be perfectly honest" or "to be totally frank," which of course means they are lying through their teeth.

There's another first-name no-no that even I occasionally

commit. It occurs when you can't remember someone's name, so you grasp for all manner of verbal fill-ins to cover your mental block. "Hey ... sweetie ... how have you been? I was thinking just the other day, I've got to give ... that girl ... a call. How's it going?" You'll say anything to avoid the proper name of the person. I have a friend who has even taken to calling people by the wrong names, just to keep the conversation flowing. His wife later calls everyone to apologize. Why don't we create a national pact, where we either wear name tags or promise to divulge our full names at the start of any conversation? Either that or prepare to be addressed as "Pal," "Honey," or only "You" for the rest of your life.

Piercing the Veil

When I was thirteen, my friend Pam and I went to Baribault Jewelers in Glastonbury, Connecticut, and had our ears pierced. It was a big deal. I remember the sound of the piercing gun, the sting of the needle, the little gold studs we bought for twenty dollars (piercing included). Men, for the most part, didn't get piercings, which is the way it should be. Once men (especially athletes and hip-hoppers) really got into ear piercing, it was all over. Somewhere along the line we started taking a "manifest destiny" approach to our own bodies. It is not unusual for people to deface themselves with multiple piercings (the "ear spear"!). And how comforting that "ear plates" are no longer just for Ben & Jerry's scoopers! Now we hardly blink when we see piercings through eyebrows, noses, belly buttons, tongues and . . . a-hem . . . private parts. (Not that I've actually seen the latter!) Of course, people who take pride in their "hole-y" approach to body design insist they are merely communicating their individuality. Okay, but last time I checked, pincushions don't usually have a message.

Spitters

The other day, I'm sitting in traffic and a taxi driver in the car ahead of me opens his door and proceeds to spit into the crosswalk. Before the light had changed, he did it again. Whatever was rattling around in Omar's throat is now presumably on the floor in someone's foyer or on the rug in a child's bedroom. It's too horrible to think about. Camels behave better. And yes, I am glad that the European Tour fined Tiger Woods for spitting on the greens. He was violating the code of behavior that the players had agreed to uphold. When he hawked up a loogie on the twelfth green during a golf match in Dubai, a BBC announcer called it "one of the ugliest things you will ever see on a golf course . . . somebody now has to go behind him and maybe putt over his spit. It doesn't get much lower than that." (Woods's ex, Elin Nordegren, might disagree, but I digress . . .)

Maybe we should revive the use of spittoons and make people carry them around their necks. Not only is spewing phlegm onto public spaces disgusting and illegal in many places, it is also hazardous to our health. There is a reason that spitting was outlawed at the turn of the century. Our forefathers knew that TB and other diseases could be spread by contact with that glob you hawked up on Avenue E.

The best is someone who, caught in the act of spitting, cites an ancient custom as justification for this filthy habit. Ariel Scheib, writing for the Jewish Virtual Library, reminds us that it is an ancient Jewish superstition "to spit three times in reaction to something that is especially good or evil." The figurative "pooh, pooh, pooh" will suffice, thank you very much.

Adjusters

Some people should reconsider the size of their underwear. For some reason, there are men and women who constantly feel the need to adjust themselves in public. I have personally witnessed women entering a party or some other event who, with no shame, reach into their décolleté and jostle their cleavage. The motion is rarely elegant and looks like a clumsy breast exam— ending with an inspection in front of a reflective surface to ensure that a tenuous "balance" has been achieved. Other women tug at the elastic of their underwear in a vain attempt to resituate it over their backsides. One does not wish to imagine the condition that thong is in after a day of readjusting.

Men are the worst offenders. Some seem drawn to their crotch before engaging in any activity—as if it were that log that contestants rub for luck before singing at the Apollo. Some Major League Baseball players have made genital adjustments into a pregame show. Other men touch their anatomy as regularly as the rest of us scratch our heads or rub our noses. It is an ugly habit. If your groin requires that much attention, might I suggest some flea and tick spray.

Pickers

Is it just me or do you notice that more people seem perfectly content to pick their noses in public than ever before? I was standing in a checkout line the other day and in the aisle next to me was a kindly-looking, heavyset, middle-aged man. While waiting, I casually glanced in the man's direction. In horror, I averted my gaze quickly. Three quarters of his index finger was jammed up his right nostril. He must have hit the mother lode because that digit made several revolutions before finally emerging. Once he pulled it free, he had the gall to inspect his findings. What accounts for this sheer lack of basic etiquette? If a tissue is not readily available, is it really that much of a strain to wait until you get one? Or, alternatively, is it possible that one can become a snot addict? In other words, you're so hooked on the "high" that you feel when that pesky booger is finally dislodged that you don't notice that several people are staring aghast at your archaeological expedition?

For some, the spelunking runs from top to bottom. It starts at the nose and ends with the toes. I was once on a theme park shuttle while on vacation. Seated across from me, a woman took off her sandal and began to pick cheese from between her toes.

Now I can personally attest, there truly are picking jobs that no American should be willing to do.

Ear Divers

You can be pretty much anywhere and cross paths with an ear picker. I write this while on a treadmill at my local gym (I know, I deserve to go catapulting off the back of the conveyor belt). A man on a stationary bike in front of me, wearing a sweat-drenched undershirt, just used the corner of said shirt to dig into his right ear canal. Then, to determine whether he had excavated the wax treasure within, he examined the shirt closely. Unsatisfied with the results of his makeshift Q-tip, he stuck his pinky in the same orifice and rooted around with a ferocious urgency. Does he think that the gym setting somehow exempts him from basic rules of human grooming? Orangutans preen with more discretion.

Teeth Suckers

"Tsk, tsk, tsk"... That is the sound of people who, after gorging themselves at a restaurant, proceed to suck air between their teeth in a futile attempt to loosen food particles. The most persistent of whom (like a lobbyist I sat near once) improvise dental floss using the edge of the menu or a random book page. If this is not successful, they don't ask for a toothpick, but continue the conversation while intermittently sucking on that piece of filet mignon trapped between their molars. "Laura, it's really wonderful the way you . . . tsk, tsk, tsk . . . have taken to the airwaves with a message that touches so many people . . . tsk, tsk, tsk . . . your mission is so important . . . tsk, tsk, tsk . . ." At first, I wasn't sure if he was offering pity or had Tourette's. I didn't realize what was happening, until he reached for the menu insert and proceeded to slide it between his caps toward the gum line.

The Grazers

Walk into any big grocery store and you'll see them: the grazers. These are the folks who treat the free samples in the aisles as a midday meal. They can make a lunch out of cheese cubes, Swedish meatballs, frozen pizza squares, and hummus spreads. You're not supposed to belly up to the sample table and make yourself at home. The toothpick is there to skewer a single sample, not to be loaded up like a kebob. The fact that their double-dipping is unsanitary is of no concern to them. They are focused on their prey—the mound of mini crab cakes under the plastic dome cover.

The idea is to take one morsel and move along, but the grazers have perfected their technique. They walk up and announce to the poor table custodian, "Hey, so, what have you got there?" This fake discussion buys the Grazer precious time. As the poor woman goes into her sales pitch, the Grazer is already scarfing down samples. He then doubles down: "Hey, honey, you've got to try this fish!" Soon the Grazer's spouse shows up and begins to dine. By the time they are finished, only the dill garnish is left on the plate. Once the samples are exhausted, they either guilt the table attendant into hauling out more grub or they move on to the next grazing station—as if Sam's were their own personal cocktail party. Of course, they never buy. That would violate the Grazer's Code of Ethics. They live to disprove the old adage: "There's no such thing as a free lunch."

Ice Chewers

I'm sitting in an elegant Manhattan restaurant. White linen tablecloths, waiters in jackets, finger bowls, the whole shebang. The friend I am dining with is sharing some of the most hilarious stories I have heard in years. The waiter fills our glasses with water and ice. Within seconds, my tablemate stops talking and is now crunching on the ice in his glass. He chews with such gusto, he looks like Nanook of the North, trying to liberate something from a small glacier.

No joke—there is a not-so-secret society of ice addicts who consume ice like hors d'oeuvres. There has to be a quieter way to fracture a molar. Friends who are ice-obsessed tell me that they actually choose restaurants based on the ice they serve. According to the *Wall Street Journal* the gold standard is created by ice machines like Chewblet, Nugget Ice, or Pearl Ice—which produce feathery, fast-melting ice. The fast-food chain Sonic rates high among ice connoisseurs, who, I kid you not, order only cups of ice at the drive-through. I don't care how feathery or chewable the ice is—it is meant to support polar bears, oil rigs, or to be left to melt in a glass—not to be gnawed by humans. Snow cones excluded, of course.

Worse than chewing ice is when people turn it into a type of musical instrument. Their recital begins with rattling of the ice in the glass, chomping down on a cube or two, then spewing the remainder back into the glass, so it may be twirled again. Spare us the symphony, and save some tooth enamel for your old age.

Body Shots

Watching someone on a bad bender when you are totally sober is uncomfortable enough. Watching that same person at a sleazy bar, and treating her body orifices—or someone else's—as shot glasses is repulsive. Welcome to the world of body shots, where it is perfectly acceptable to slurp booze off a total stranger's midriff or backside. You wouldn't want to be caught dead in the establishments that promote this unsanitary and debasing practice. It involves a man or a woman lying atop a bar and having salt and alcohol poured into a body indentation (cleavage, belly buttons . . . I'll stop there). Their friend, or at times a stranger, then laps up the hooch to a frenzy of flashbulbs and caterwauls. The trashy entrepreneur Joe "*Girls Gone Wild*" Francis made millions by convincing bombed coeds to engage in the practice, often while totally topless.

I was giving a speech in a college town a few years ago and headed out afterward to a local hot spot. We ran into some sorority sisters during the last night of rush. One of the more degrading rites of passage involved drinking body shots off blotto locals. One pledge was told to lick alcohol off the prodigious gut of a guy who could have been the stunt double for the late Chris Farley. Displays of intimacy should be kept behind closed doors; displays of infamy like this one should never occur. Looking at the hairy boar lying on the bar I thought, you could not shave and scour him enough for me to even order a gin-and-tonic at that bar, much less do what that simpleton is doing.

Like so many modern practices in our culture, this one humiliates the participants, turns intimacy into sport, and makes otherwise normal people do stupid things in an effort to appear cool. You want to be cool? Try alpine skiing. It'll give you a genuine thrill, and you might be able to show pictures to your kids in years to come—without shame.

Unwelcome Charity

Some people make being charitable more difficult than it should be. I ran across one such man about seven years ago outside my favorite Capitol Hill eatery. He was living on the street, obviously down on his luck, and held a sign that read "Will work for food." So I asked our waitress to pack up an extra turkey sandwich, chips, and a Coke. He was hungry and I was going to make him feel better, if only for a few minutes. I couldn't step past him one more time and consider myself a caring person.

Little did I know, that Mr. Scruffy not only didn't want

"work," he didn't want food at all. When I tried to hand him the paper bag holding the food, he started screaming at me and crying, "Help!!! Get away from me! Leave me alone, woman!!" Poor dear. He took the bag and threw it in traffic. Rejected by a homeless person—er, a bum. That was a low point.

Undeterred, I tried this routine with other street people—er, hobos—a few more times. I have had hot coffee thrown on my legs, fresh-baked croissants pitched in the trash, and my business card torn up and spit upon. (I gave one woman my number and told her to call me if she wanted help finding a job. She started railing about conspiracies at CBS. I couldn't really disagree with her.)

I've learned my lesson. Christmas shopping in midtown Manhattan last year, I came across a man with a sign reading, "I Just Need Beer Money." For his refreshing honesty, I flipped him a twenty.

Arming the Audience

Don't you hate contrived fist pumping at a concert? Do the producers of the Super Bowl halftime show really think we're that stupid? No, we don't think all those people spontaneously ran onto the field to demonstrate their spur-of-the-moment enthusiasm for the "musical performer's" glow stick dance.

Then there are the people who wear classic concert shirts of the band they are going to see. Hey dude, we already assume that if you spent three hundred dollars for nosebleed seats at a

Rolling Stones concert, you're a fan. We aren't impressed by the frayed '81 *Tattoo You* T-shirt and don't need to hear your critique of the set-list in the concession line.

I will never forget how my last Springsteen concert was marred by a guy seated behind me who insisted upon screaming out requests in between songs. "Boss!! 'Born to Run'!!" As if there were any possibility he wouldn't play it.

Usually the people who shout out their favorite songs at concerts are the same ones who insist upon singing along—flat and off key—with every lyric. And it's even worse when they forget the lyrics. The lyrics of "Hungry Heart" are "you lay down your money and you play your part," not "you play me honey and you broke my heart"! Face it, Baltimore Jack, glory days have passed you by.

Singer on Board

Speaking of unwanted crooning, if you plan on singing in your car, do it when you are alone. Unless I am sharing a ride with Placido Domingo, I don't want to hear any singing from the driver. It is a type of torture to be imprisoned in a vehicle with a motorist who not only believes he can sing, but then accompanies himself with an air guitar or steering wheel drum set.

I was on a long drive with one of these offenders a few years ago. To distract me from the fact that he had no idea where we were headed, this driver elected to play Elvis tunes. Soon the car was a rolling karaoke chamber. I nearly engaged the airbag when he started speaking along with the long monologue in "Are You Lonesome Tonight." Stop wondering, I'm not lonesome. It's just that your singing is loathsome. Suffice it to say, he couldn't play the part of Burger King, let alone the King of Rock and Roll.

Mercifully, I don't think these people can hear themselves. They have become so accustomed to their melodic slaughters that with the volume of the CD player cranked up, it must sound like music to them. I now travel with my foam insert ear protectors. They work perfectly at the gun range and in taxis where the cabbies are belting out the latest hit from a Bollywood soundtrack. The only thing worse than a stranger in close proximity singing off key and botching the lyrics is when the stranger is warbling some indiscernible tune in a foreign tongue. Car manufacturers could solve this crisis for us. Forget the mute button on the radio—we need a mute button for the drivers.

Flagging

I hate themed, decorative house pendants. You know what I mean: the nylon flag with the Old English Sheepdog, the colored eggs for Easter, the Christmas snowman, or worst of all, the college football team flags. Aren't the bumper stickers and the matching jerseys you and your family wear each Sunday enough to convey team loyalties? The only flag that should ever be flying outside your home is an American flag or the flag of the branch of the armed services you served in or wish to support.

Night Drops

People who let their dogs off the leash at night should be fined or perhaps made to stand in dog poop for twenty-four hours without moving. Under the cloak of darkness, these dog owners feel empowered to do things they would never dare do in daylight. When Rex the Chesapeake Bay retriever happily leaves a nocturnal fecal mound on my lawn, his master of excretory disaster doesn't leave so much as an apology note. I have caught him in the act and shouted out, "Hello, Jared!" He looks around and pretends he cannot hear over the music playing through his iBuds.

By the time I wander out for the last stroll of the night with Lucy, I'm not only picking up her droppings, but those of other night depositors, too. I tote along a pocketfull of plastic grocery bags to hold the brown lawn sculpture left by the Great Dane down the street. I'm thinking of installing motion-activated floodlights on my front lawn to discourage the mammoth nightfall excreta. Perhaps the solution is a nutritious dog treat—one that creates an individualized color-coded glow. That way, we can easily identify the canine culprit the next time his leash and his bowels are released in the night.

Muffin Tops

If you are overweight, you should not be humiliated by stupid thin people, but nor should you humiliate yourself. So do not try to sandwich your beautiful big self into a pair of skintight hiphuggers. It does not make you look thinner, and my Lord, is it unattractive. Yet there are young women who each day shimmy themselves into jeans far too small for their frames. I imagine these poor women greasing up their legs with body lotion just to slide into those hip-hugging, body-shaping asphyxiation slacks. The final display is often referred to as a muffin top.

Against that pernicious and calumnious nomenclature, I rise in defense of true muffin tops. Muffin tops are tasty, desirable, and always a delight to see. Women (or men) who turn themselves into human bratwursts in an attempt to look fashionable fail miserably. It seems like only yesterday when I was a college junior, lugging my own muffin top across the Dartmouth Green.

Ladies, even if you manage to squeeze yourself into the jeans, the cellulite will find a way out and up—I promise you. Not long ago, I saw a cadre of young girls in the mall. Each of them committed the double sin of wearing extra-tight jeans and snug midriff shirts. They were also sipping the new gallon-size Frappuccinos. "Muffin Top" does not begin to describe the sorry appearance of these poor girls.

If you have a tummy problem, cinching the fat in and hoisting it up over your belt is never advised. Unless you are trying to look like a Macy's Thanksgiving Day balloon trapped in a chimney, don't do it.

A quick word of advice: if after buttoning your jeans, your midsection is wider than your backside, it is time to remove the jeans and purchase a caftan.

PajamaJeans

Now they have something called PajamaJeans. For those who find jeans too confining, the infomercial claims that they "look like denim but feel like pjs." In other words, they are extra stretchy to accommodate maximum expansion. PajamaJeans are actually loungewear masquerading as jeans—leggings made to look like denim without the restricting structure. You can pretend they are jeans all you like, but if you and two friends can fit into your "jeans," they are not jeans. Those are spandex sweatpants. I can't wait for PajamaLeather, for those who want a rock star look as well as that third dessert.

When Underwear Poses as Pants

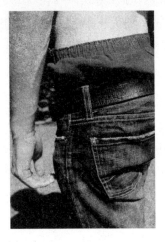

It has been going on for years: men and boys who insist on wearing their pants somewhere near the kneecaps. Aside from making them walk like penguins, this disturbing trend creates an unsanitary situation that nauseates me whenever I see it. Each time they plant their posteriors on a seat (in a theater, restaurant, or some other place with a chair you are likely to use) it is their stained underwear that makes contact with the surface. I don't care if your underwear is polka-dotted, candy-striped, or is encrusted with stones derived from the Hope Diamond itself—I don't care to see it. It's called underwear because it should be *under* your pants, not a substitute for them. If you can't remember that, just reverse the words to form the imperative: wear under.

This supposed fashion choice is sometimes called "sagging," but it should be called "gagging"—which is the likely reaction of anyone having to witness these "pants-on-the-ground" buffoons.

Some trace the style's origin to the prison system, where inmates are not allowed to wear belts, for fear that they would commit suicide. So now the un-incarcerated expose themselves in public places, while the rest of us wish we could commit suicide.

Another sagger sub-species is composed of men of a certain age and girth who wear their pants under their stomach overhangs. Their trousers defy the laws of physics, precariously perched just above their coccyx bone, secured by belts that seem like they are under far too much stress. Perhaps these guys are just too lazy to go out and buy new belts, so they keep using the thirty-four-inch ones they wore in college.

I'd like a few of you "sagger" men to drop into a Banana Republic dressing room and check out the rearview mirror. Not only do your sagging buttocks frighten children, but there are vertical stripes on your underwear that I don't think were part of the original design pattern. Please pull them up, gents, or kindly continue your "sagger" style where the trend started: central lockup.

Manscaping

Have you noticed that more men have taken to waxing their eyebrows? How can these people ever be taken seriously? Okay, if you're Andy Rooney and the eyebrows are braidable, then perhaps a trim is in order. But when you're sitting next to me in the Elizabeth Arden salon, flipping through the latest issue of *Brides* magazine, you've lost me. The actor known as "The Rock" is perhaps the best-known offender. I would almost prefer that he shave the brows off entirely.

And it's not just the perfectly coiffed eyebrows that men yearn for; they want satiny-smooth chests, too (except for Simon Cowell). When I was a kid and you heard about a man waxing, it usually involved a green jar with the word "Turtle" printed on the label. Today, men ordering a mere chest and back wax at most metrosexual spas is practically passé.

For men who want the hairlessness of a ten-year-old (and you know what I mean), they can really make a statement by getting a "he-wax." (By the way, isn't that term an oxymoron? How does going to a beauty salon to have the hair ripped off his private areas make him appear more manly?) According to a "hair re-moval" expert at About.com: "For those men who desire a totally bare bikini just ask for the 'ultimate' he-wax ($125) at Bliss Spa to get all of the hair removed in the pubic area, both front and back." Query: How much would you have to be paid to press warm wax and hair removal strips on some fat, smelly, hairy guy's no-fly zone?

What about the poor guys who have Chewbacca backs? Before they consider waxing, they should think about all the money they are currently saving on sun block. Then again, if your wife has to pass the Electrolux over your lumbar shag at the end of the day, it might indeed be time to consider a "dipping."

The Dye Has Been Cast

Gents if you are going gray, go gray. There is nothing more shameful than a man sitting in a beauty salon, his hair wrapped in aluminum foil, under a dome dryer. Nothing could be less appealing to a woman. Gray hair actually makes a man look distinguished and seasoned. Dyed hair makes him look like John McLaughlin ("Wrong!"). For whatever reason, men can never get the color right. It's always just this side of burnt orange.

One time, I had the pleasure of running into an old beau when he was getting his "color wash" applied at one of Washington's most froufrou salons. The last thing he expected to see was me sashaying up as his Chestnut Number 5 was being applied. I kicked his foot and announced loudly, "Hey, I guess this is where all the girls come to get their hair skunked." He muttered an embarrassed hello and tried to keep his focus on the BlackBerry he was clutching for dear life. As the testosterone evaporated from the room, I walked away then yelled back to him, "Once she puts in a few highlights, that is going to look super cute on you!"

Aging Hippies

Recently, I was visiting an old college pal at his law firm in Manhattan. It was a sleek, ultrahip place, teeming with well-dressed lawyers young and old. He introduced me to one of the firm's senior litigation partners, and I thought, "Now that's an attractive older gentleman!" Slightly balding with salt-and-pepper hair, he was wearing a gorgeous tailored navy suit, crisp white shirt, red Hermès tie. But then when he turned around to go back to his office, I recoiled in horror. Slinking down his back in a curly tangle was a four-inch scraggly gray ponytail, held together by tiny multicolored beads and a filthy black scrunchy. It was jarring. I know what you're saying: "To each his own, Laura!" Fine, but I have one question: do senior men with long locks think that it makes them look younger and more virile? Please. They look like a cross between Jerry Garcia and the Snow Miser from *The Year*

Without a Santa Claus. Awful! The only time we should ever see a wiry gray ponytail is on an actual pony with a chronic disease.

Manscara and Guyliner

When did it become acceptable for men to wear eyeliner and mascara? I'm not talking about the members of Green Day. I'm talking about the kid bagging my groceries, who, but for his braces, could be Liza Minnelli. When I'm checking out, I need a man who will help carry crates of bottled water to my car—not a performance by Adam Lambert.

A study in the *Daily Mail* recently revealed that more than three million British men wear makeup in public. One in ten use their female partner's cosmetics. And though American men are probably less likely to don the guyliner and manscara, as I look around, I think the Yanks are making up for lost time.

I was sitting in a restaurant the other day, and the man seated at an adjoining table kept rubbing the side of his face. As I looked more closely, I realized that he was trying to blend his makeup around the edges. It was all uneven, like he had applied it with his fingers. If you're going to wear makeup, for Max Factor's sake put it on with a makeup sponge. But gents, unless it's Halloween or you are about to perform for an arena full of your screaming fans, leave the compact in your girlfriend's purse. Russell Brand should be the object of your ridicule, not your personal makeup ideal.

The Murse

In their mission to erase all vestiges of masculinity once and for all, the fashion mavens have done away with the backpack, the briefcase, and the gym bag. The only accessory acceptable to the chic man about town is the murse. This purse-like man-pouch is all the rage in most metropolitan areas. At first, they weren't as objectionable because they were modeled on satchels you'd expect to see on a World War I infantryman. But over the last few years, they have gotten more and more . . . well, feminine. The leather, canvas, and Naugahyde man-bags are now indistinguishable from their female counterparts.

Why does a man even need a purse? A man should carry around exactly two items: a wallet and a phone. If you routinely tote anything more than that, you just might be a woman. With coin purses, brushes, makeup, tissues, and other female products, we ladies need the extra space. A man can survive with a lot less.

What a man chooses to carry his stuff in tells us a lot about who he is. Men should by nature be solid, tough, and strong (think leather briefcase)—not soft, delicate, and transparent (think macramé tote). Carrying a shimmery Dolce & Gabbana clutch is not going to endear you to a woman—we won't think you are cool or hip. But if you play your cards right, we might just loan you a set of matching pumps.

The Mirdle

Don't even try to convince us that you are wearing a "compression shirt" or an "athletic body shaper." Where I come from, it's called a girdle. Guys, I sympathize about the brutality of gravity, but please join the men's liberation movement and go bra-less.

Companies like Equmen, Sculptees, and Spanx have all unveiled male gut cinchers. For a mere seventy-nine dollars you too can skip those exhausting sit-ups and cut right to the six-pack. All the models sporting these "mirdles" have chiseled abs and sculpted chests. I doubt if the customers look like that. Wouldn't you love to see some of the three-hundred-pound, beer-bellied buyers trying to squeeze themselves into these spandex tops? It might tighten up what's there—the way a sausage casing shapes the lard—but muscle tone is beyond the capabilities of even the mirdle.

Gentlemen, if you want toned abs, get a gym membership and do it the old-fashioned way. Leave the "compression shirt" to

Aunt Sadie—she'll know what to do with it. She's been wearing one for years.

Men's Skinny Jeans

Levi's has forever disgraced its rugged, mining camp roots. The company recently released a brand of super-tight, skinny jeans for men. They call them "The Ex-Girlfriend Jean" and describe them thusly: "Remember the girlfriend with the great style? Here's a tribute to her—a fit that's super-snug all over, an update of the five-pocket classic that's as skinny as it gets."

When did men's fashion turn into a "tribute" to the opposite sex? Does this mean that if the guy can't take his eyes off the girlfriend's miniskirt and high heels, we can expect him to be cross-dressing next season? There is something seriously wrong with all this. I've often heard it said that men would "like to get into a girl's pants," but this is ridiculous. And given their anatomy, why would men ever want to wear "super-snug" pants? These things look like leggings. Unless you are the lead dancer at the Bolshoi, just stick with the loose-fit khakis, Joe.

Two (Bare) Feet Under

The Woodstock generation is (rightly) blamed for spawning harmful moral and cultural pathologies—a soaring divorce rate, promiscuity, degrading art and music, and government dependency. But a particularly noxious by-product often overlooked comes in twos—as in, feet. Bare feet. I am too young to remember the contemporaneous media coverage of Woodstock, but the images of the throngs, the filthy, muddy bare feet have left an indelible footprint on my mind.

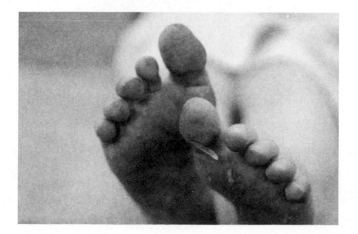

This marked the time when it became "cool," a sign of anti-establishment thinking, to boast bare feet in public. The baby boomers were essentially telling their parents and the rest of civilized society that they didn't give a darn. And it's been down (foot)hill ever since. Uncovered feet are the ultimate lazy man's fashion statement. When putting your socks and shoes on becomes too taxing, it's fair to say you're an indolent slob.

Don't get me wrong. Feet are perfectly reasonable as body parts go and are certainly useful in keeping us upright. But let's face the cold truth: as a general rule, women's feet are not as gross as men's. Now of course, there's always the woman with the hammertoe, bunion, or cracked heels in sandals sitting next to you on a plane, or using your armrest for her unsightly and malodorous extremities. (Oh, and girls, toe rings don't help, they just focus more attention on that which most of us prefer to avoid.)

As for men, God bless them, their feet should be concealed unless they're at the beach, a pool, in bed, or at home. Toddlers excepted. Who are these people with foot fetishes? Have they never glanced down, let's say, in a restaurant to see a bedraggled twenty-something in bare feet, filthy leather flip-flops, and gnarly yellow toenails? It's an appetite killer. Just when you are about to dip into the Camembert, you imagine that the creamy stuff you are about to spread on the Triscuit is toe cheese. The hairy little trolls at the bottom of most ankles trap all manner of debris and dirt, especially when nails are left unclipped and begin curling over the toes themselves.

These days, however, most men don't think twice about showing up barefoot almost anywhere—the grocery store, airport, class, and for the most sophisticated—church. This is the ultimate in "flip-flop" mentality, and is often accompanied by other fashion horrors such as baseball caps, floppy sweats, baggy shorts, or ratty T-shirts. To be critical of the barefoot phenomenon invariably elicits this response: "Remember, Jesus wore sandals!" To this you say: "Once you start turning water into wine and healing the blind, you will get a sandals exemption. Until then, keep the dogs in their doghouse!"

Tattoos

Whenever I talk about this issue on my radio show, I am inundated by conservatives proud of the American flags on their biceps, or the Ronald Reagans emblazoned on their thighs. You could tattoo the entire Declaration of Independence on your back, and it would still be more moronic than patriotic. And please don't call it "body art." Tattoos are not only disgusting and low-class, but as you age, they change shape. The cool eagle tattooed on your shoulder at age eighteen? By age forty-five, it looks like a seagull with leprosy. If only that bird could fly far, far away . . . off your body! And gals—the tattoos in the intimate areas are especially desperate. Any guy who needs a road map by that point is well beyond your ability to help.

The Liberal College Slacker/Protestor

You can always recognize the lefty, twenty-something college protestor. They were crawling all over the Wisconsin union protests of 2011 and are the mainstay characters at anarchist rallies in the United Kingdom. "Protestor chic" is definitely its own look:

- *A Dirty Knit Ski Cap.* This standard-issue cap looks as if it has been left in a New York City snow thaw and recently recovered on the floor of a public bathroom. Whether it's on a head or not, coagulated hair grease maintains its domed shape at all times.

- *A Soul Patch or Other Irregular Facial Hair.* Another distinguishing characteristic of the college protestor is that annoying hair growth just beneath the bottom lip. (This applies to both male and female rallygoers.) Why would anyone equate this ugly growth with the soul? Yes, Howie Mandel, I am speaking to you: *No deal!* If protestors aren't wearing a soul patch, they allow random facial hair to sprout out all over their cheeks. The pattern often resembles the latest weather model on Doppler radar.

- *A Woven Pullover.* A common fashion choice of the protestor is the woolen hooded Aztec number that looks as if they forgot to weave the thing. I believe they just rip the wool directly off the sheep and attach a hood to it. If you look closely, you can still see the burrs and twigs from the farm sticking out. Each time I see them, I want to protest—their clothing!

- *Sandals.* For some inexplicable reason, whether the sun is shining or there are three-foot snowdrifts, protestors feel bound to show up in Birkenstocks or flip-flops. Are these the only shoes they own? Some punish us by displaying their yellowed, fungus-ridden nails (perhaps if you wore normal shoes your toenails wouldn't be six inches thick).

Common modes of transportation for the professional protestor include: folding bikes, scooters, and union buses. Regardless of how they get to a rally, expect them to exhibit pungent body funk once they arrive.

Vehicular Manners

There should be a manners manual for parking. The rudeness of people in parking lots is worse than Bill Maher at a morning church service.

Offender #1: Parking Spot Thieves. These are the idiots who know darn well you have been sitting with your blinker on for ten minutes, waiting for granny to retouch her makeup and back out of her spot. Then the moment she vacates the space, these people cut you off, quickly zipping in. I make it a habit to stare them down after they pull this stunt. Many are so humiliated they slink out of the passenger door, and into oncoming traffic, just to avoid my glare.

Offender #2: Dingers. You've walked out of the mall and returned to a vehicle covered in dings, dents, or scratches. The offender is usually the car formerly parked next to yours. This is not a "bumper cars" ride at Busch Gardens. Learn to park without doing bodywork to someone else's vehicle. Incidentally, the Dingers are the same people who are asking for your insurance number and speed-dialing the cops the moment you so much as kiss their bumper.

Offender #3: Non–Parallel Parkers. In and out, back and forth . . . Then if they do get part of the car into the space, they repeatedly inch backward and creep forward in a futile attempt to straighten out. Meanwhile, traffic is snaked back to the interstate waiting for this moron to parallel park. If you don't know how to expeditiously parallel park, find a spot that doesn't require the skill or ask someone to do it for you. And if you are driving a land yacht, please realize your car will not fit into that spot marked "compact," no matter how many times you try.

Offender #4: The Cigarette Danglers. You are in bumper-to-bumper traffic. The weather has just turned nice, so you roll down the window to get some fresh air. That's when the person idling in front of you decides to hang a lit cigarette out of his Cutlass Supreme. The smell soon inhabits your car and stays there. If I wanted a ride that reeked of smoke, I would have reserved a rental. Keep your smoke to yourself. One time a dangler tossed his lit cigarette into my path as I walked across the street. I picked up the butt, threw it back into his car, and said, "I think you dropped that."

Bumper Stickers

Why is it that the first idiot to cut you off in traffic is always the one with the "Coexist" bumper sticker on the rear window of his car (usually a Subaru, Prius, Volvo, or Honda Fit)? Likewise, whenever I see someone with a "Perform Random Acts of Kindness" sticker slapped on his rear window, I keep my distance. He's usually the poster child for road rage, and terrorizing the elderly and small animals. I have also had it with those "My child is an honor roll student" stickers. Darling, how are we to know that your child isn't one step away from being featured on an MSNBC *Lockup: San Quentin* special? I'm waiting for the first honest parents who slap a "My child is a lazy, entitled slob" on their rear window. The "Visualize World Peas" slogan is still making the rounds and still makes no sense. And don't give me that "My other car is a Porsche" nonsense. Your other car is a bike. Now get moving, and stop distracting other drivers with your vapid bumper-philosophizing.

The "New" Stupid

I am tired of people rhetorically attempting to alter reality by adding the term "new" as a prefix. You've heard it before: Gray is the new black. Fifty is the new thirty. Sixty is the new forty. No, sixty is the old *old*. We're getting older. Get over it.

In politics, some describe America's diminished status in the world and our skyrocketing debt as the "New Normal." This is the most self-defeating phrase ever created. It was devised by people who prefer to pass bad news off as a way of life. No, it is not the New Normal, it is the Current Situation, which we need to strive to improve. Though these people may well be the New Stupid, which used to be called the Old Delusional.

The Grand Invitation

The other day, I was opening the mail when I came across a six-inch-tall box in the shape of a pyramid. It was brushed in gold and had a small door with a tab that read, "Open here." When I pulled the tab, it split the pyramid in two, and glitter, stars, and Mylar King Tuts fluttered all over my carpet. It was an invitation to an Egyptian-themed party. Standing in the pile of glitter litter, I felt like Mubarak after the riots. Whatever happened to the single embossed card as an invitation?

When you have to send a carnival attraction in the mail to get people to come to your party, it's probably going to be a lousy affair. What kind of lunatic sends out themed Mylar figures that they know will spill all over the carpets and furnishings of the people they claim to like? As I was trying to read the invite (between the faux hieroglyphs), my dog Lucy started eating King Tuts off the floor. Not only did I refuse the invitation, I decided to send the hosts a bill for the carpet cleaner and the vet. Thanks for the invite!

Early Wake-up Call

I was born late, and I have carried on that tradition throughout my adult life. It's not something that I am particularly proud of, but there are worse things—such as being early. When I throw a dinner party and specify that we'll begin cocktails at seven o'clock, it doesn't give you license to show up at 6:35 p.m. The first words uttered by the early arrivals are always something like, "I hope it's okay that we're a little early!" Of course, a proper hostess says, "Why, of course! Come right in! Wonderful to see you!" My subliminal reaction, however, is "Good, I'm glad you're here so you can take out the recycling, pick up the Legos in the living room, and vacuum up the dog hair before the *real* guests arrive." Those twenty-five minutes that they just stole from me are critical, but the early birds are oblivious to the chaos they have caused. (They're usually the haggard parents who wanted to escape their own homes as early as possible.) "Honey, I think you forgot to put eyeliner on both eyes," an old friend pointed out after she crashed my house almost a half hour before our dinner. Gee, thanks. I was in the middle of applying my makeup when she rang the doorbell! These early birds shouldn't get the worm; they should be served the worm.

3

Popped Culture

There are so many problems in our popular culture, I could have devoted the entire book to the topic. Celebrity sexcapades, trashy reality television, disgusting lyrics, and bad movie remakes combine to put our popular culture on a steep downward trajectory. The fact that adults breathe this in is bad enough. But when children absorb this toxicity, our entire society is in jeopardy. Look carefully at the trends in television, music, film and food, and you'll catch a glimpse of our future. I know you'd probably prefer to avert your gaze, but none of us can afford to ignore what is happening around us.

Media mania

This year marks my fifteenth anniversary in cable news. I've worked in one capacity or another for just about every news network in America. I've been a guest, a host, a guest host, and a substitute host. I've been hired, fired, and almost rehired once by one of the same network presidents who fired me. I've seen talent and executives come and go like mysterious rashes. I've seen networks stumble through new slogans, new show concepts, new graphics packages, new lineups, and new sets. So I write the following with a uniquely informed perspective.

Co-Hosts from Hell

When Kathleen Parker was recently (and ill-fatedly) paired with Eliot Spitzer on CNN, I felt her pain. It is the rare exception when co-hosts genuinely like each other. Think about it—in most cases, theirs is a construct conceived in some executive office somewhere, not born out of a real preexisting rapport. Then, suddenly, after a pilot or a few rehearsals, the camera light goes on and . . . presto! they are supposed to be chirpy and cheery and engage in the sort of back-and-forth that takes years for normal people to develop. When I wake in the morning or go to bed at night, the last thing I want to see is some male-female duo engaging in saccharine, meaningless banter:

"Well, Melissa, in our local news roundup, the zoo is celebrating the birth of its first baby kangaroo in years."

"Awww, how cute, Alex, but let's *jump* to the weather first," she quips. (Alex laughs unconvincingly.)

"Thanks, guys. Speaking of Australia, this month's temperatures are *down under* the seasonal average," says the meteorological correspondent.

Since so much of the news is entertainment these days, why not go for the real entertainment factor? Why not have these news "buddies" tell each other how they really feel?

"Thanks, Alex, for that fascinating tidbit about the zoo's new addition. That gets me thinking—you have a lot in common with the little joey. He lives and nurses inside the pouch of his mother . . . kind of like your relationship with station management."

"Oh, is that supposed to be funny? Hard to tell, by your facial expression. After all that Botox, your face looks like it belongs on one of those hikers found frozen to death along the ascent to Everest."

All Graphics, All the Time

It used to be that just Bloomberg television was crowded with graphics, charts, multiple stock tickers, etc. But now all of the cable channels look that way. Twelve years ago, I complained to the management at MSNBC when the news ticker was added to my daily show, *Watch It!* "Distracting" and "cluttered" are words that I used, but my complaints fell on deaf ears. They kept adding more on-screen doodads. When I was told the show was canceled, I asked my boss, "Have you broken the news to the graphics?"

Today we see more information on a screen than ever before: weather, price of commodities, promos for upcoming shows, horoscopes, and occasional recipes from Paula Deen . . . they're all up there. Call me an old fogey, but when I want to watch the news, I don't want it to look like the Vegas Strip. I'm waiting for the launch of a cable news network that prides itself on having no programming at all—instead the screen would be filled only with moving, pulsating, spinning, flashing graphics. We could call it NNN—The No News Network. But then again, we already have MSNBC.

Fighting for Ratings

Is there any way we can call a global cable news moratorium on the airing of those hideous fight videos? You know the grainy, badly lit iPhone videos of teenage miscreants brutalizing each other that have become a cable news fixture. Admit it, your eyes linger if the combatants are of the feminine persuasion. Given the prevalence of these YouTube smackdowns, you'd think that every time you went to the grocery store you'd be accosted in the meat section by some crazed woman wielding a leg of lamb. But after an extensive, six-month investigation, I've determined that the most infamous girl-on-girl assault videos seen over the last few years can actually be traced to a single staged brawl filmed in Studio 2B at 30 Rockefeller Plaza. My attempts to determine which cable executive authorized this production have been un-successful. I'm awaiting the *Dateline* follow-up investigation.

The Tyranny of the "Strategists"

The word "pundits" includes the word "pun" (joke) and "dits," which sounds like "ditz." Maybe that's why I never liked to be described that way. Equally irritating and overused is the word "strategist." "Republican strategists" and "Democratic strategists" are all over cable television. Most of them seem to pop up out of nowhere. They are certain their on-air brilliance will soon allow them to ditch the title "strategist" for "contributor," which means they actually make money off the deal. "Democratic strategist" Joe Smith has usually: a) not strategized for anyone unless you count helping his friends land chicks at happy hour; and b) believes he can be the next Bill O'Reilly. Same deal with the Republican "strategists." Their total political experience is the summer they spent working at the RNC during college, licking stamps, or writing constituency letters. When I was starting out in cable news, I'm sure I was introduced as a "strategist." I felt guilty about it and wondered what would have happened if I insisted that they label me something like "anxious, out-of-work lawyer." Well, I "strategized" my way into working for MSNBC, CBS, and now . . . the best of all by far . . . Fox.

Breaking News

This Just In . . . it's not breaking news. It's the same story that ran last hour. The only thing new is the anchor reading the tele-prompter. The only thing breaking is the pancake on his face.

HD

If I wanted the American public to dive into my pores and swim, I'd attach a mini diving board to my face. There is no way a woman would have ever invented high definition. It's cruel. Now makeup artists (always the most interesting and fun people in television news) tote makeup guns that are supposed to "even out" your skin tone for high definition. But I notice they use the liquid makeup dispersant only on men and women of a certain age—and I'm one of them. When I'm on camera, I long for the days of spotty UHF signals and dial televisions with rabbit-ear antennas.

Oh, and even if you enjoy watching stuff on HD, by the time you actually find the HD channel on your station guide, the pro-gram's usually over.

A Sucker Born Every Minute

I'm not a great sleeper. Never have been. I usually wake up at least once in the middle of the night, and when I can't fall back asleep, I sometimes make the classic mistake of turning on the television. Why is the first channel that pops up always one of those infomercials starring a self-proclaimed real estate guru? And whom do they think they're fooling by filming their cheesy pitches against a backdrop that looks like the old *Larry King Live* set? These self-proclaimed entrepreneurial visionaries are usually "interviewed" by an aging, flamed-out television personality. It broke my heart when Hugh Downs, formerly of ABC's *20/20,* popped up to partner with one of these hustlers.

These late-night snake-oil salesmen tease us by promising that they have "proven strategies" and "methods" to make you tons of dough—and you never have to leave your house! Featuring testimonials from other supposedly "regular people" who hit pay dirt by using these super-secret "techniques," these scammers talk in circles about their "program" and its "easy-to-follow steps." It can be strangely addicting to watch. "For just three easy payments of $19.95, you'll start discovering the strategies that can change your life forever!" "Triple your net worth in your spare time!" "Learn the tricks the pros use!" Please. It all begs the question: if he's such an expert in his industry, why is he spending time in a particleboard studio talking to a former TV host who is now pretending to be a current one?

Head Coaches, Head Fakes

Maybe it's not fair to put "life coaches" in the same circle of Dante's Hell as the aforementioned flimflam artists, but they're awfully close. Life coaching is big business these days. The

coaches claim to use "core principles" to help people with relationships, business, and even fitness.

Years ago, I almost bought the Tony Robbins tapes. He's done
so well with this claptrap, that he basically owns one of the Fiji
islands. While attending Robbins's "Life & Wealth Mastery"
sessions at his luxurious Namale Resort, Spa, and "University
Campus," grown men are reportedly driven to tears. I can sympathize. One night after I caught one of his infomercials, I had an
unsettling dream. In pitch darkness, I was being chased through
a tropical rain forest. All I could see coming up behind me was
a giant set of snapping teeth. They kept crying out, "Unleash the
Power Within! Unleash the Power!" I could never watch one of
his infomercials again.

The Worst Commercials

No one really likes commercials, but there are some that raise a
visceral hatred in me.

Like millions of families, you're watching *American Idol* with
the kids, when in the middle of the show, a young girl wearing
nothing but her underwear interrupts the broadcast. Suddenly,
the room falls silent. The children's eyes—especially the boys'—
are riveted to the images on the screen. You tuned in to watch a
talent show and got more "talent" than you ever expected. One
minute, the *Idol* kids are singing a medley; the next, boobilicious
is coming at you. The message of the Victoria's Secret ads is clear.
If you girls want to get noticed, lose the clothing and turn on

the sexy. And guys, this is the female ideal: a slinking sexpot in lingerie. There is nothing wrong with lingerie, but the sales pitch makes it look like every "Miraculous" bra comes with its own stripper pole. Their new "Bombshell Crush" line promises "Instant cleavage. Instant lift. Instant attention." How empowering.

And I dare you to watch a major sporting event on television without a Viagra ad popping up (no pun intended). That middle-aged man soaping his car (I've never seen so much foam) is already weird, but when the woman walks over and beckons him inside the house, it's just plain gross. As the suds drip off his car's fender we hear that sultry voice-over: "Viagra can help guys with all degrees of erectile dysfunction. Ask your doctor if your heart is healthy enough for sex . . . Seek immediate medical help if you experience an erection lasting more than four hours." Parents across the country scramble for the remote. Too late! Rather than enjoying the rest of the game, they spend time answering questions they didn't plan on answering for years. "What's 'sex,' Mommy?" or "What's an 'erection lasting'?"

Not to be outdone, a Viagra competitor, Cialis, takes a more subtle approach. These ads feature a couple in separate claw-foot bathtubs on a beach, a cliff, or perched on some other outdoor vista. First, why are these people in tubs—and what exactly is the message here? Does Cialis promise to put a porcelain barrier between partners? Millicent Badillo, who spent three years developing the ads at Grey Worldwide, told the *New York Times*, "It's associated with all the good things [people want]: intimate moments, taking your time, being stress-free." I don't know about you, but if I were naked in a bathtub on a public beach, I doubt if I'd be "stress-free."

Nearly as painful as the ED advertisements are those for medications to supposedly alleviate "Low T" (testosterone). Even if the ads are too understated to prompt questions from the kidlets, must the rest of us be subjected to this? (And if "Low T" is truly a medical condition, let's hope it's covered by the health plan used by members of Congress.) This ad campaign must have been designed by a female ad executive as payback for decades of uncomfortable "feminine hygiene" commercials.

The other commercials I detest are any featuring talking babies. The moment an infant starts to speak, I make note of the product and avoid it like the plague. Seeing those demonic, animated baby mouths is enough to give me the croup.

Dancing with the . . . huh?

Nicole Scherzinger, Michael Catherwood, Steve-O, Louie Vito. If you don't know who these people are, don't feel bad; neither does anyone else in America. All of them were contestants on ABC's popular *Dancing with the Stars*.

Ingraham Rule of Television Casting: if you are neither a dancer nor a star, you do not qualify to appear on *Dancing with the Stars*. Many times I can't even focus on the dancing, because I am trying to figure out who the purported star is. They should really have a star graphic hovering above the party who is supposed to be the celebrity.

Kathy Griffin may live her life on the D-list, but many of these *DWTS* contestants don't even make the alphabet—and they can't cha-cha.

The Most Boring Things on Television

In addition to golf, there are a couple of television genres that are among the most tedious and boring things ever recorded. At the top of the list are fishing and hunting shows. I love people who cling to their guns and I'm not anti-hunting, but come on. I know it's going to sound elitist, but watching two scruffy guys in quilted camo whispering to each other in a blind, strategizing about how they're going to take down Bambi's daddy, is a bore. Unless the deer are armed, there is absolutely no drama here. These men have high-powered weapons deadly and precise enough to kill the flea on the deer's back, much less the poor deer. Try killing a wild animal with a spear or a bowie knife, and I might tune in.

And how about those how-to oil painting shows that look as if they were shot in 1979? These shows could survive only on PBS. (Your tax dollars at work!) Why is it that the artist (you remember him, the guy with the frizzy hair) never finished the painting of the mountainscape? During one of his interminable dissertations on impasto, he said, "We don't have mistakes here, we just have happy accidents." At least he got the "accident" part right.

Visiting the Dregs of Society

Cable subscribers spend thousands of dollars welcoming some of the most revolting members of the gutter into their dens, kitchens, and bedrooms, courtesy of certain premium cable channels. HBO began the descent to the bottom of the cultural wasteland with its groundbreaking *America Undercover* documentaries, which pulled back the veil on the lives of strippers, porn stars, and hookers. The network's highest-rated documentary series of all time took viewers inside the Bunny Ranch, an authentic Nevada brothel. *Cathouse: The Series* soon gave way to a scripted HBO show about a male prostitute. *Hung* is, believe it or not, a comedy, according to reports (and no, I have not seen it), concerning a basketball coach who turns to prostitution to make ends meet.

Before long, Showtime caught the male prostitution bug (or should I say disease). Its new show is a reality series called

Gigolos. It follows a group of struggling male prostitutes in Vegas as they make their rounds. The *New York Times* recently described the show as "bluntly pornographic" and asks the sensible question: "Who in the world are these seemingly ordinary people . . . who consent to have cameras record their sexual and legal deviances?" When the *New York Times* starts getting judgmental, you know you're really in the sewer.

Given this creative trajectory, it is only a matter of time before Showtime does a reality show based on its hit series *Dexter:* "Butcher Daddies: The Softer Side of Serial Killers." Each episode will feature a harried ax murderer trying to get the kids off to school and finish a presentation for work, while planning a quickie homicide or two.

The Only Losers Are the Kids

Isn't it time to admit that we have an awards show problem? The Oscars, the Grammys, the Tonys, and the Emmys used to be special. It was all so glamorous. But now every television network and cable outfit has to hand out its own deformed statuettes and ugly plaques. We now have the ESPYs, the MTV Awards, the VH1 Awards, the BET Awards, and the TV Land Awards. We should have known it was only a matter of time before a children's network got into the act.

The Nickelodeon Kids' Choice Awards features an annual display of fresh crudeness and stupidity all its own. The 2011 edition did not disappoint. I don't know about you, but I would prefer if my kids did not think it a good idea to hurl green slime at people for laughs. Nickelodeon thinks otherwise. Whoever produces these stupid Kids' Choice Awards parades a stream of celebrities onto the stage and under the slime faucets, until everyone is covered in green goo (an apt image of our pop culture). Heidi Klum, Josh Duhamel, and Snoop Dogg all took turns getting slimed. Not that it mattered to the kids—since they didn't know who these people were to begin with.

For those youngsters with a refined sense of humor, the Kids' Choice Awards presented a group of celebs competing in an "armpit fart" contest. Then suddenly from the air, Willow Smith (ten-year-old daughter of Will & Jada) came flying into the arena on cables like a Wallenda. Was I terrible for thinking, "I hope the director of *Spider-Man* the musical isn't involved in this production?"

The question is: why do Hollywood A-listers like Johnny Depp, Justin Timberlake, and Jim Carrey subject themselves to this kind of stupidity? They do it for the same reason they do everything—to push product! Depp had an animated film, *Rango,* in theaters when the Kids' Choice Awards aired. Jack Black was there to flack his forthcoming *Kung Fu Panda 2* sequel. As host of the show, Black even did a couple of televised talkbacks with his animated (panda) alter ego, who at one point threw lo mein at Britney Spears. Yes, she, the Black Eyed Peas, and Miley Cyrus put in appearances, too. The gangly and unfunny Brit Russell Brand also popped in—or should I say, hopped in—to promote his movie *Hop.* This animated

Easter film had the distinction of mainstreaming porn to the SpongeBob set. In *Hop,* Brand plays a reluctant Easter Bunny–in–waiting sowing his wild carrots. At one point in the movie he visits the Playboy Mansion where that master vocal talent Hugh Hefner informs him that they allow only "sexy bunnies" into the homestead. "I can be sexy," the little bunny says. Just the sort of catchphrase we all want to hear our grade-school children repeating, isn't it? (By the way, Hef and the Playboy brand make another appearance later in the movie.)

Whether through children's award shows, animated features, or guest spots on *Sesame Street,* celebrities now extend their brands to the little ones wherever possible. It's all about selling things and reaching the young demo. How long before Katy Perry shows up at the Huggies Infants' Choice Awards, wearing an overnight and a onesie?

Celebrity Causes

If you happen to find yourself on Capitol Hill, I hope you have a cell phone camera handy, because chances are you will bump into a celebrity. Every other day, some Hollywood star is testifying before one congressional committee or another. From the looks on the senators' faces when the stars walk in, you'd swear that John Adams had come back from the dead. What makes these people experts in anything other than acting? (*See* L. Ingraham, *Shut Up & Sing.*) Learning to mouth other people's words does not suddenly equip you to offer your half-formed opinions on the federal budget, the environment, or the state of African nations. But don't tell Ben Affleck.

Talk about a daredevil. The actor recently testified before Congress, urging more U.S. aid to the Democratic Republic of the Congo. He first visited the Central African country in 2008. While it's admirable that Affleck set up a nonprofit to help the people of Congo, a few goodwill tours and a photo op do not make him an authority on African affairs. And George Clooney, unless you are willing to trade that villa on Lake Como for a hut in the African veld, spare us the lectures and the White House emotings over the terrible state of Sudan. What happened to activists who actually live among the people they speak for? I was recently invited to testify before a congressional committee on China's human rights abuses because I devote a lot of time to the issue on my show. However, since I don't consider myself a China expert and haven't spent time there, I declined.

Leonardo DiCaprio has a green foundation that exists to "secure a sustainable future for our planet and all its inhabitants." That would not include human inhabitants, apparently. Though he encourages petitioning the Chinese government to "save the tiger," there are no DiCaprio petitions for saving the millions of young girls who are exterminated each year by the Chinese government's "One Child Policy." Wake up, Leo, tigers don't buy movie tickets, and their cubs won't expand your fan base. I also didn't notice Leo registering any protest when the Chinese authorities recently rounded up artists and writers for daring to criticize the regime. I guess the need to distribute films in mainland China makes cowards of them all.

Stars are also good at creating buzz in Washington for issues that have absolutely no constituency. Take the actor Mark Ruffalo, who recently came to D.C. to make the case against fracking. To most Americans, fracking sounds like a curse word. Ruffalo wants to stop the hydraulic fracturing used to drill for natural gas (fracking). You see, the actor's home in upstate New York is according to *The Washington Post* "in the path of a gas drilling rush" and the fracking could disrupt his rural tranquility. Mark, the *kids won't be all right* if they have no way to heat their homes this winter.

Confessions of a Desperate Celebrity

Is it really necessary for us to know that Shannen Doherty and Camille Grammer (Kelsey's ex) suffer from inflammatory bowel disease? Unless they had signed up to do live, televised colonoscopies, who was going to find out? And what difference does it make to their viewers or fans?

The tabloid culture is fed not just by paparazzi stalking celebrities for photos and scoops. It's also fed by the celebrities themselves, who willingly divulge the most intimate details of their lives for profit and attention. Mackenzie Phillips should have taken another "day at a time" to consider whether we really needed to know that she had a consensual, incestuous relationship with her father, musician John Phillips.

Does anyone think that Ashley Judd is a better actress since she shared details of her troubled childhood, including alleged sexual abuse in her latest book, *All That Is Bitter & Sweet*? Not to be outdone, her mother, Naomi, and sister, Wynonna, subsequently appeared on *The View* to disclose that they too had been sexually abused—and that more family secrets would be revealed on their new docu-series, *The Judds*, on the Oprah Winfrey Network. How convenient. I don't know about you, but at this point, *I* feel abused!

Boundless self-exhibition has become the standard in our culture. If they want to launch a book or a film, it is now mandatory for celebrities to serve up every detail of their lives for public consumption. While it may make us feel morally superior in the checkout aisle to scoff at the wrecked lives on the tabloid covers (*schadenfreude*), there is a cultural toll. Our children are watching and listening. They are being taught that the more personal information you make public, the more popular and successful you can become. Things best left in the confessional or the therapist's office have now become fodder for public conversation. Discretion is dead today, and privacy is an afterthought. The truth is, we don't really care or need to know who's sleeping with whom, what drugs they are doing, or whether they've checked back into rehab. Dirty laundry, no matter who owns it, should be kept in a hamper and washed in private.

Bring on the Distractions

Remember when singers could hold a stage on talent alone? We valued someone with a real voice and a connection to the material. Think of Frank Sinatra, Elvis, Sarah Vaughan, Ray Charles, Stevie Wonder. The overwhelming majority of today's pop stars are not fit to carry their mike stands.

Why is it that nearly every major "singer" today needs to be flanked by a battalion of dancers bumping and grinding on stage with them? One possibility—they need something to distract us from the fact that their talent is limited to lip syncing and shaking their cans. And do these big acts not have enough money in the wardrobe budget to buy full costumes for their backup dancers? I am convinced that if Saran Wrap ever goes out of business, Lady Gaga and her crew will come out wearing only rouge. But Gaga has a lot of competition. Enter Britney Spears.

Spears represents the sort of overproduced, titillating performer who quickly reaches her expiration date. Her recent album, the lackluster *Femme Fatale,* demonstrates that whatever was once there is no longer operable, and all the gyrating, sweaty dancers and girl on girl kissing can't resurrect this tired act.

Spears did a big rollout of her album with a live performance on *Good Morning America.* The number titled "Hold It Against Me" had pyrotechnics, flashing strobes, lurid dancer-wallpaper, and absolutely no life. Spears lip-synced the lyrics to a track and executed her dance moves with all the elegance of a stroke victim on Valium. Undeterred by her low-energy performances and subpar vocals, the shameless Britney later appeared on MTV, where she explained the roots of her artistic genius—her creative childhood: "I was just like . . . really kinda . . . like . . . just really creative and just really just, y'know, like that." She should run for office.

When they are not re-creating tableaus straight out of a peep show, "singers" like Katy Perry rely on an entire city of backup singers. There are so many vocalists belting the melody out behind Katy Perry that you wish she would step aside and let them actually take center stage. Though Katy did put in her time. She was previously a backup singer for that legendary performer Miley Cyrus. You see, genius does beget genius.

Please, Master Just One Thing

It is all the rage today to be a "crossover performer," one who can sing, dance, act, write, direct, produce, decorate and cook. But what happens when the crossover artist can barely master the craft they are known for? Gwyneth Paltrow comes to mind. The fetching actress who won an Academy Award for *Shakespeare in Love* hasn't fronted a hit movie since. Now, I realize that she is married to Coldplay's Chris Martin, but that doesn't mean she can sing. Still, Paltrow headlined a movie, *Country Strong*, about a boozed-up singer on the road to recovery, and sang all the vocals. Promotion required an obligatory stop at the 2011 Country Music Awards.

Paltrow sang the title track before a live audience, awkwardly holding an unmiked guitar that we were supposed to believe she was actually playing. Couldn't she have just presented an award? After hearing her, it is no surprise that Atlantic Records called off plans to record a country album with the chanteuse. No matter, she later popped up on *Glee* to sing the Cee Lo Green magnum opus "Forget You," (a slightly cleaned-up version of "F#@k You"). It's now a Paltrow standard. She would sing the song again at the 2011 Grammys, backed by a cast of Muppets. At least she found duet partners worthy of her vocal talent. If the singing career doesn't work out, Paltrow can always fall back on her lifestyle website and cookbooks (have the personal chef and nannies gotten author credit yet?).

Another crossover offender is Jamie Foxx. He too is an Academy Award winner and also like Paltrow, must believe that this entitles him to punish us with his crooning. I know that he is one of a rarefied group to win the Oscar and score a number-one album on the *Billboard* charts—but like Shakira's hips, my ears don't lie. Jamie, you are a comedian. Your apex was when you were wearing a dress on *In Living Color*. Wanda was intriguing. Your singing is not.

To prove how ill-suited he is to be a musical performer, Foxx sang a duet with will.i.am on last season's *American Idol*. Flanked by a drum line and a legion of carnival dancers, the pair endlessly repeated, "I want to samba / I want to party." I felt sorry for Mr. Black Eyed Pea, who actually does have some (though not a lot of) talent. Next time you're asked, just say will.i.am not singing with this man!

The term "triple threat" used to refer to an entertainer who could sing, dance, and act. Today it refers to a performer who threatens to show the audience just how lousy he or she is in all three disciplines.

Young and Foolish

Neither Justin Bieber nor Rebecca Black can sing. There, I've said it. These two kids should thank God for synthesizers. I've heard warmer vocals on a voice-message greeting. The moment Bieber hit puberty, it was all over. "Baby, baby, baby . . . go back to Canada, Canada, Canada!"

As for Rebecca Black, I don't care if gazillions of people have watched her "Friday" music video on YouTube. Two words: it's free. Her fan base is those who watch cute cat videos and trampoline accidents.

> *Annoy-in' annoy-in' (yeah)*
> *Annoy-in' annoy-in' (yeah)*
> *Dumb. Dumb. Dumb. Dumb.*

Filthy Lyrics

If music reveals the heart of a culture, ours is in cardiac arrest. Every week, there is a new dirty lyric set to a beat. Each is as profane as it is obvious. Just when you thought it couldn't get more explicit, along comes another stupid act begging for attention. As a sign of just how low things have gotten on the music scene, here is a bit of Rihanna's latest ditty "S&M":

> *Sticks and stones may break my bones*
> *But chains and whips excite me . . .*

How a woman who is perhaps best known for having been physically abused by ex-boyfriend (and studio demolitionist) Chris Brown could sing lyrics like this defies explanation.

Justin Timberlake and Timbaland's "Carry Out" is another beauty. This one equates the female body with a drive-through. Note: I could not find one feminist group that objected to this song or its misogynist message:

> *Take my order cause your body like a carry out*
> *Let me walk into your body until it's light's out*

Step aside, Irving Berlin. I don't know what is more gross—the lyrics or the video. Cosmetically enhanced breasts and women squatting predominate. And why is it that performers like Timberlake, Jamie Foxx, or Usher can't perform without grabbing their crotches? Is there a pitch correction device down there? By the sound of things, I doubt it. So if it's all the same to you, please either join a Major League Baseball team or sing the song without fondling yourselves, okay?

For all the ugliness in pop music, there are still real romantics like Enrique Iglesias. The Spanish moss has fallen far from the tree. His father sang "To All The Girls I've Loved Before." Enrique has now given us "Tonight I'm F#@%ing You."

> *Please excuse me I don't mean to be rude*
> *But tonight I'm f#$*ing you*

Then we wonder why teens are degrading themselves on cell phones, acquiring STDs, and are more crude than ever. They are simply following the example set for them by these paragons of talent and sophistication. I liked Justin better as a Mouseketeer, when the only things he was grabbing were his plastic Mickey ears.

Auto-Tune to the Rescue

Ingraham Rule of Thumb: The more desperate and flailing a "singer's" hand motions, the worse the singing. I refer to the ladies with the "raining fingers" whose digits mirror their wild vocals as they run up and down the scales in a desperate search for the right note. One hand lives on their earpiece; the other executes the rain gesture. Tie her hands behind her back, and Mariah Carey might not be able to produce any sound at all—which could well be an improvement.

Then there are the chest pounders. These are the singers who finish a song and then beat their chests in a victorious gesture. Like it was a special honor for us to hear them hit the high note.

Think about it: not even silverback gorillas pound their chests with the frequency and ferocity of Celine Dion. And it also won't cost you two hundred bucks to see them.

There are other artists who have not been able to hit a high note for decades. No matter, they've devised a host of strategies to mask their vocal shortcomings. Sometimes they lustily launch into a song, and as the notes get higher, they simply begin talking. The high notes are thrown away, almost treated as an imposition upon their performance. Other singers refuse to admit defeat. As they get into the upper register, a determined vibrato kicks in that would make Ethel Merman blush. They strain to hit something, and occasionally land near the right note. Still other singers have been yelling for so long, they've forgotten that there ever was a right note. Rather than be too specific, vocalists like Steven Tyler or Liza Minnelli explode into a full-on wail that encompasses several notes and keys.

Singing should be beautiful. No shouting, machine-gun vocals, or dancing fingers are needed or welcome. Now, please, pass the Bose noise cancelling headphones.

Shilling Abroad

When you travel to other countries, you realize that many of our favorite stars, who wouldn't be caught dead appearing in a commercial at home, are more than happy to play pitchmen abroad— if the price is right. Showing up in a commercial Stateside could dim the luster of an A-list star, but picking up a few million in foreign lands, why not? And who's looking, anyway? Most of the stars sign ironclad contracts to keep their humiliating foreign adventures away from domestic eyes. Do these stars think that they're the only people who travel?

I was shocked during a recent trip to Russia to find that Bruce Willis's picture is as ubiquitous as Lenin's once was in the old Soviet Union. His campaign for Russia's "National Bank Trust" features a photo of Willis with the caption "Trust, it's just like me, only a bank." I still don't get the billboard, but perhaps someone will in the 170 Russian cities where it is displayed. Bruce reportedly took home a cool $3 million. Why not just sign on with

Wells Fargo here at home? And what exactly is the connection between Benicio Del Toro and Russian ice cream sticks?

If you happen to visit China, you will soon see Leonardo DiCaprio in a commercial for the Guangdong OPPO Mobile Telecommunications Corporation, a cell-phone company. It is one of the most lucrative international celebrity deals out there, and according to NBC, it netted DiCaprio $5 million for his trouble. Though this isn't Leo's first trip to the foreign ad market. He has previously appeared in offshore campaigns for Suzuki and watchmaker Tag Heuer. And he's not alone.

Cameron Diaz can be seen peddling cell phones in Japan. Salma Hayek is flogging Campari. Brad Pitt pushes blue jeans and mobile phones in Asia. Nicole Kidman induces Italianos to buy Nintendo DS. Ben Stiller appears in a Japanese Kirin beer ad surrounded by cheerleaders in a football stadium (Pity that Godzilla didn't show up on the field). Kiefer Sutherland can be seen in a *24* send-up for a product called Calorie Mate, while Charlize Theron sensuously slips into a bath for Lux. George Clooney never met a foreign ad he didn't like. Clooney is the poster boy for Honda in Japan, Omega watches in Italy, Martini throughout the European Union, and most recently, Nespresso coffee in Germany.

For those who find all of this unbecoming and cheap, you are not alone. Russell Crowe told *GQ* that he considered the offshore celebrity endorsements a breach of faith with the audience: "I don't use my celebrity to make a living. I don't do ads for suits in Spain like George Clooney or cigarettes in Japan like Harrison Ford. And on one level, people go: 'Well, more fault to you, mate, because there's free money to be handed out' . . . to me it's kind of sacrilegious."

That's a bit of an overstatement, but it is odd that these celebs are so ashamed of their endorsement gigs that they have to hide them overseas. Message to the A-listers: there is now this thing called the Internet. Whether you are at home or abroad, no matter the language, your fans know exactly what you are doing. Just admit it, you're capitalists just like the rest of us.

It Was So Good the First Time

While peddling their remake of *True Grit* in Europe, Joel and Ethan Coen told the *Guardian* that John Wayne and his memorable Academy Award–winning portrayal of Rooster Cogburn in the original movie had no influence on their film. Wayne was "an irrelevancy," in the words of the Coens. Funny, after you watch both versions back-to-back, despite the directors' protestations, they seem to have borrowed far more from Wayne's portrayal than they'd like to admit. The Coens claimed they drew their inspiration from the 1968 novel on which the original film was based. That may be true, but when Jeff Bridges is riding both guns a-blazing with horse reins in his teeth, exactly the way John Wayne performed the scene, it's hard to see the difference—or why a sequel was necessary. The truth is, for all the interesting performances and atmospherics created by the Coens, their remake pales next to the original. It is a film interesting only in relation to its predecessor. Without Wayne's indelible performance, no one would have cared about a *True Grit* reboot. But at least the remake took no liberties with the original story. Other movie classics don't fare so well, especially when politics enter the scene.

Hollywood has a real problem with communists—they hate to show them in a poor light. In 2004, Jonathan Demme remade the classic 1962 hit *The Manchurian Candidate*. As the name indicates, the original film dealt with a group of American soldiers who are captured by the communists, taken to China, and brainwashed. A particular soldier is later hypnotized to carry out a political assassination. The original, starring Frank Sinatra, Angela Lansbury, and Laurence Harvey, was a spellbinder. In the Denzel Washington remake, the communist plot is totally scrubbed, and to justify the title, an awkward story adjustment is made. This time, the soldiers are no longer taken to Manchuria, but rather are brainwashed by Manchurian Global, a corporate giant. That's right, a capitalist corporation is cast as the bad guy, since we all know that businessmen are much more menacing than a communist nation. Oh, okay.

A new version of the camp classic *Red Dawn* has similarly been reimagined by timid filmmakers. The 1984 film followed a resistance movement of teenagers who repel Soviet communist invaders on U.S. soil. The update by MGM originally recast Red China as the enemy. But hoping to sell the film in the lucrative Chinese market, they reedited the movie to the tune of $1 million and made North Korea the bad guy. Scenes were reshot and Chinese symbols were scrubbed digitally—along with their U.S.

box office hopes. North Korea? Why not make Malta the aggressor nation?

Great comedy remakes can also be destroyed by poor casting and even worse scripts. Anyone who saw Steve Martin in a Pink Panther movie or Russell Brand's attempt to banish the memory of Dudley Moore in the dreadful remake of *Arthur* will know exactly what I am talking about.

When they're not ruining great films, Hollywood turns bad TV shows into movies. Was there truly an outcry for an *A-Team* theatrical feature? *Charlie's Angels*? How about *The Dukes of Hazzard*? It won't be long before *Who's the Boss* and *The Nanny* hit the big screen. But I'm holding my breath for the *Diff'rent Strokes* remake with Jaden Smith and George Clooney.

The Living Dead

Walk into a bookstore, flip on the TV, or hit the Cineplex and it's obvious: the undead are among us. Our derivative culture has resurrected the creatures of the night, and I for one am looking for the holy water.

Since the time of Bram Stoker's *Dracula*, the vampire myth has been repackaged for successive generations. But with the *Twilight* saga, HBO's *True Blood*, and the endless movie and TV knockoffs like CW's *The Vampire Diaries* (teen dracs) and ABC's ill-fated suburban vamp series *The Gates*, it is clear that vampires are here to stay. The question is: what's different about this latest incarnation of bloodsuckers? In the Stoker era, vampires were

evil predators to be feared and vanquished. No more. The Twilight and Sookie Stackhouse books have turned them into mis-
understood heroes with an unsatiable hunger—sort of a Charlie
Sheen with fangs.

Max Wixom, a New York publicist and member of a vampire
reading group, described the vamp chic this way to the *Daily
News:* "We're moving Vlad away from (a) boogey monster to
a romanticized figure that's beautiful. We're taking it to the
next level of embracing the darkness." Just what we need: kids
"embracing the darkness," creating more moral confusion than
already exists. The new vampire trend has convinced the young
that bloodsucking, predatory creatures of the night are romantic
ideals to be emulated, while truly good people are squares and
idiots. Nice going, Sookie.

Then there are the zombies. At least vampires have intel-
ligence and are at times morally troubled by their conditions.
Zombies, on the other hand, are ungainly, mindless creatures
looking for a quick snack—in many ways a mirror image of the
audience. No wonder they are so popular. Zombies have risen to
new prominence in feature films like George Romero's *Survival
of the Dead* and on the hit AMC series *The Walking Dead.* It is
estimated that no fewer than twenty-one zombie pics are set for
release in 2011 alone. They're even invading bookstores.

Lacking an original idea, publishers have begun to pillage and
profane great works of literature by simply inserting zombies
and vampires into the plotlines. So now we have Seth Grahame-
Smith's *New York Times* bestseller, *Pride and Prejudice and Zom-*

bies, in which, Elizabeth Bennett slays zombies and ninjas, when not dealing with Mr. Darcy. Jane Austen is doing somersaults in her grave. Now copycats are everywhere: *Little Vampire Women, Mansfield Park and Mummies, Sense and Sensibility and Sea Monsters,* and *Jane Slayre* are filling bookshelves. Seth Grahame-Smith, who started the monster mash-up genre, decided to forsake the classics and immerse himself in history. His latest work is *Abraham Lincoln: Vampire Slayer.* Somebody has been watching one too many episodes of *Buffy* in his spare time.

These undead creatures not only suck the blood out of their victims, but they've now turned our entertainment anemic. Isn't it time to close the lid on the coffin and focus again on the living?

Cupcake Chic

What is so special about cupcakes that people will pay three to five bucks apiece for the things? So much for the bad economy . . .

Boutique cupcake shops have opened all over the country, in part spawned by the success of the TLC show *DC Cupcakes.* This is one of those reality shows capable of glazing not only cupcakes, but also your eyes. *DC Cupcakes* follows the intensely boring lives of Sophie and Katherine, the two sisters who founded and run Georgetown Cupcakes in Washington. The shop sells more than five thousand of the frosted treats per day, according to the show's website—and I have witnessed the lines of people at all hours of the day myself.

Okay, the Georgetown Cupcakes are good—but so are Little Debbies. I just can't understand what's so fascinating or unique about cupcakes. And absolutely nothing could induce me to stand in line, in D.C.'s freezing cold or blazing heat, to buy high-priced small cakes. Unless you are doing breast and lung cancer breakthroughs with that coconut mocha crème, I'm not interested.

Still cupcakes are, for the moment at least, a huge business. Sprinkles, which began in Beverly Hills (and claims to be the first cupcakery), now has eleven locations, and Crumbs Bake Shop in New York recently went public. Crumbs was sold for $66 million and will soon go from 35 cupcake shops to more than 200 nationwide. I mean, they're not exactly making ambrosia in these shops. It's a box of Duncan Hines, a couple of eggs, and some food coloring. Looking past the cupcake lines, the hype, and the reality show, one thought keeps coming to mind: Krispy Kreme. After a meteoric rise, that stock fell quicker than their patrons' backsides.

Homemade cupcakes are better anyway. No lines. A fraction of the cost. And a few drops of food coloring, and you have your own "Red Velvet"!

Lingua de Starbucks

For decades, Starbucks has been overcharging Americans for java. I don't know about the star part, but they've got the bucks down pat. At what other establishment would you hand over ten dollars for a cup of coffee and a muffin and gladly return the next day? I am among the guilty.

Starbucks has become a way of life for millions—a mania fueled by caffeine addiction and the need to clutch a status sym-

bol. "No McDonald's Café here, baby. I only drink Starbucks."
And you pay dearly for the privilege.

Where else would you give up four bucks a day for one drink
and not think twice about it? Over ten years, that's more than
twenty-two thousand dollars. Is that mocha latte really worth
a car? I guess it depends on what you get for your dollars. Any
organization that measures out quantities of ice and milk per
customer with the chemical precision of Starbucks has to be
making a killing. Those green lines running around the plastic
cups are not for decoration. They are there so that the college
dropout preparing your drink will dole out only the prescribed
amount of liquids and ice. Order an iced chai tea, for instance,
and Starbucks fills half the cup with ice. They then add a splash
of chai flavoring, a few drops of milk, and it's done. Four dollars
for a cup of ice surrounded by a few ounces of tan milk. For that,
you could have purchased a whole gallon of milk. Ditto for my
favorite latte.

For some reason, I always end up with the trainee who has
never steamed milk before. Inevitably, it takes her fifteen minutes
to get the froth in my cup just right. Or maybe she's just stalling
to give me more time to peruse the overpriced CDs and coffee
accessories. No matter how bored you are as you wait—let me
offer this caution—don't touch the scones. In terms of flavor and
appearance they taste like particleboard and look like cow pat-
ties. Heck, all the pastries at Starbucks could be exhibits at the
Smithsonian. There is something antique about them—they're
like old *Let's Make a Deal* props. I can't decide what irks me most

about the Starbucks experience: the lousy pastries, the prices, or the lingo.

Only at Starbucks would perfectly normal people refer to a cup of decaffeinated coffee with skim milk as a "No Foam Grande Skinny Decaf Latte with No Syrup." The most exasperating part of the trip is their penchant for announcing not only what you ordered, but also all the ingredients in the cup.

"Laura, your Venti Soy Chai Mocha Non Fat Frappuccino with no whipped cream and two Splendas is ready." By the time they finish announcing your order, you could have whipped one up yourself. My friend Raymond is so finicky that he can't just order the house standard; he has to radically adapt the recipe to suit his taste. I know Raymond is in the store whenever the barista yells out "Skinny, green tea Frappuccino, hold syrup, extra ice, nine scoops of matcha powder." English translation: Five bucks for a cup of green crushed ice.

Would You Like Some Chemicals with Your Coffee?

Call me a purist, but I don't like flavored coffee beans—I feel like retching at the mere smell of "hazelnut" coffee brewing. So imagine my horror when I perused the dairy section of my local supermarket recently and came upon a row of products called "International Delight" creamers. The dizzying variety of flavors on the shelf (clearly inspired by Starbucks' success) made my eyes start to spin: Dark Chocolate Cream, Caramel Macchiato,

Southern Butter Pecan, English Almond Toffee, Chocolate Caramel Irish Creme—and my favorites . . . the "Limited Edition" Almond Joy and Cinnabon flavors. Apparently, coffee with sugar is no longer good enough. We need our cup o' joe mixed with a double scoop of ice cream and other assorted candies and desserts.

By choosing a sugar-free "Skinny White Chocolate Mocha," we're supposed to feel better about what we're pouring into our coffee. But I'll take the cholesterol of regular old heavy cream over that chemical soup any day. Maybe it's all just a way to mask really cheap, tasteless coffee. (Radio stations are known to have horrifically bad coffee and stock either powdered creamers or the flavored individual servings.) News flash: You're not fooling anyone. Nescafé and Taster's Choice isn't made any more gastronomically sophisticated by adding these creamer chemicals. If I want a Superfund site with my coffee, I'll go to the Love Canal.

Flash Mobs

Stay home, mobsters. The public does not want to be cast in your *Glee*-ified world. If you must sing publicly, join a chorus or audition for a musical. My mall or grocery aisle is not your personal recital hall. Maybe we should consider filing a RICO action to protect society against this kind of mob activity.

4

Relation-Slips

We all have them. We can't live without them—though some-times we wish we could. Relationships are wonderful, vexing, infuriating, intoxicating, fulfilling, and often completely un-fathomable. How we relate to our parents, children, significant others, friends, coworkers, neighbors—and yes, our pets—tells us a lot about who we are and where we are going. Far too often, we are just too lazy, annoyed, or selfish to give relationships the proper care and feeding they require. At other times, we give them more of our energy and attention than they deserve.

The Family Feud

Don't you just hate it when people say, "Family is the backbone of civilization"? (Wait, didn't I just write that in my last book?) In fact, the way some parents treat their children, and vice versa, it can be more like the "backside" of civilization. Of course, we all appreciate that without family, the whole shebang comes crumbling down.

There are folks who really seem to have it all figured out—husbands who treat their wives like queens, wives who are selfless and unfailingly kind, children who are a delight to be around. But once you step off Waltons' Mountain, you realize that families are like every other time-honored institution—they have their moments, but are also marked by rivalries, backbiting, and seething resentments. All of these need our attention. So let's get started.

Mother-Daughter

What is it that makes teenage daughters act so horribly toward their mothers? I was one, so I know. Nothing my mother could do was right—her purse was old and ratty, she didn't have the right shoes, she had the same winter coat for ten years. Of course, Ms. Bratty didn't realize that her mother did without so she could pay her college tuition and buy her all that horrid Laura Ashley clothing that was so trendy. Now that I'm a mom, I understand how aggravating it must have been for her to deal with my ingratitude. Most moms sacrifice for their kids, and most kids don't fully appreciate it.

Not that moms are perfect—they have their issues, too. How many times do you remember hearing "By the time I was your age, I. . . ." Or "When I was a kid, things weren't so easy. . . ." Or "Just wait until you have to have to earn a paycheck and put food on the table!" We all heard these golden oldies and rolled our eyes at the time. Today we repeat them to our own kids. Can't both sides call a truce?

Children are genetically programmed to ignore these words; and let's face it, parents, it really doesn't make us feel any better saying them. A more effective approach might be: "Okay, sure, you can blow your Christmas money on a Hermès purse, as long as you realize that you will be paying for your first college semester's room and board."

Then there are those other mothers who pride themselves on being "best friends" with their daughters. My mom was too old-school for that. She had me in her mid-forties, and the concept was totally foreign to her. Mothers were mothers—not pals, not buddies, not girlfriends with their daughters. I remember being jealous of the girls who seemed to have the more modern relationship with their moms. They didn't have to suffer through the indignity of having boyfriends see their mother standing in the bay window with her hands on her hips whenever they turned up two minutes past curfew. Now as a mother myself, I intend to handle things *very* differently. I would never stay at home worrying about where my daughter was. After all, the private investigator tailing her will keep me updated on her whereabouts.

When Parents Attack

Something happens when parents retire. One day they're giving you advice about your career, love life, and child rearing; the next they're asking for directions to the drugstore and want you to take them there. Adult children often feel ambushed by the parental role reversal: "How did this happen?" they ask themselves. "They ran businesses, fought wars, managed hundreds of people, and suddenly they're helpless."

Age has a way of making all of us children, which partly explains the parental transformation. The other explanation is revenge. After decades of being ignored or openly defied by their children, I think some parents just make the decision to turn the tables and let the kids taste a bit of their own medicine. Grandma and grandpa also have lots of time on their hands ... time to find fault, time to correct your parenting, and time to ignore all your counsel.

"Kid'll never get potty-trained that way," a friend's mother recently announced at a family gathering I attended. My friend was taking her little boy to the bathroom every couple of hours, much to the chagrin of grandma. "You need to park him on the potty for several days. It's a full-time commitment," she lectured. "But you're the big woman of the world. You've got all the answers. I know you've read those parenting books and all ... What

do I know? I only raised five kids. Forget I said anything. Just keep doing what you're doing. Get used to it, because you'll still be doing it when he's ten!" After that my friend wanted to lock Granny in the bathroom for "several days."

At a Thanksgiving dinner I attended once, the entire party had just cut into the stuffed turkey when the hostess's parents began a loud discussion at the other end of the table.

"Boy, this stuffing tastes nothing like yours, Marion. It's dry as Mojave dust. Did you give her your recipe?" the father practically shouted.

"Yes, I gave her the recipe. This is my recipe, isn't it, Suzy?"

The hostess nodded, embarrassed.

The mother continued: "I thought so. But it's okay. You had more important things to do when you were *young*—like running around with those Ryland boys. By the way, Bobby Ryland married that Patricia from your cheerleading squad. Patricia's

Sunday roasts are to die for. Darling, do you have a steak knife for this turkey?" Every Thanksgiving after that, my friend went to the Bahamas—without her parents.

One of the most precarious moments in our relationships with our parents is when they seek our advice. I remember one of my radio show callers telling me once that his mother had asked him whether she should continue driving. He had already come to the conclusion that it was time for Mom to relinquish her keys. He told her she could get around with his assistance and by using the shuttle at the retirement community where she resided. Suddenly the mother became enraged: "Who do you think you're talking to?! I'm a grown woman; I don't need you to take me anywhere. My question was about the future, not the present. I can still drive just fine." Her son realized he had stepped on a "senior IED." "Oh, of course, Ma, you're a terrific driver, and I just thought—" Then his mother gave him whiplash. "Well, maybe you *should* take me to my hair appointment on Saturday. Not that I'm taking your advice, but parking's a nightmare over there. Honey, my appointment's at four o'clock, so let's leave no later than two-thirty, because you never know, we could get into an accident. It could be raining. And my girl's very busy on Saturdays—so be here on time."

If you didn't fear that your own children would follow your example, tell me you wouldn't leave grandma at the hair salon *permanently*.

Boomerang Brats

According to a Pew Research Survey, 13 percent of parents with grown children permitted their kids to move back in with them in 2009. The so-called "boomerang kids" left the nest for college, and the moment things got rough in the real world, ran home to Mommy. You know what they say about boomerangs? If you don't duck, they can kill you. Ditto for boomerang kids. Duck, Mom, duck! Change residences and leave no forwarding address. Sell the house the minute you drop them off at the dorm. Just whatever you do, don't let them back in.

Mom and Dad are just starting to rediscover each other and enjoy the tranquility of the house when slacker boy returns. Suddenly, the romantic dinners for two are made-to-order dinners for three—featuring all of Junior's favorite dishes. Mom's craft room is now a bachelor pad, her old quilting table littered with

Taco Bell wrappers. She's in her mid-sixties and once again finds herself bending over to pick up his dirty socks and underwear. How can life be this cruel?

I've heard the arguments: actually the economy is to blame; the parent-child relationship will be stronger as a result; it's a passing phase. In some cases, that may be true. In other cases, this grown man is the worst kind of moocher: the kind who uses that lethal combination of guilt and shared genetics to worm his way back into his parents' cushy home. Thomas Wolfe was right, you can't go home again—or you shouldn't, except on holidays. After eighteen years of toil, parents need a few peaceful years to enjoy hobbies and rekindle romance. They don't need another adult in the home padding around the kitchen in flannel pajama bottoms, asking "Ma, did you know we're out of Red Bull?"

Friends who have welcomed their kids back home (and successfully moved them back out) offer this advice: set firm rules, give the kids an eviction deadline, and make sure that they are gainfully employed or actively pursuing work. So many parents have welcomed children back into their homes to live with them, it will be interesting to see, years from now, if their kids return the favor. I'm looking forward to witnessing the emergence of boomerang parents. Now it's your turn, Junior! Mommy likes dinner at six sharp and cocktails at five. And keep the noise down in the mornings, will ya?

Bent Tree, Twisted Neighbor

One windswept afternoon, years ago, an elderly neighbor showed up on my porch in a housecoat with one of those plastic hair protectors over her head.

"It's windy out here," she squawked. "Did you realize that your tree is leaning?"

What exactly, I thought, did she want me to do about it? Unless my tree has uprooted itself and hopped the fence onto her property, I shouldn't be pestered about its curvature. I can barely manage my own posture, let alone that of the old oak in the yard.

"You know, that tree could fall on my house," the neighbor said. Hey, Mildred, that's what homeowners insurance is for. Leaf me alone, lady.

The Permit Trap

They seem so benign, even sweet, when they show up at your door with their clipboards and pens in hand. The neighbors have come to convince you to support the addition they're hoping to tack on to the back of their house. Without the signatures from a majority of the adjoining neighbors, they can't get a permit.

"We need a little sunroom for the kids to play in on cold days. It's really a small addition, Laura," they say. "Construction shouldn't last more than three and a half to four weeks, tops." It all seems innocuous enough, and gee, they were so nice to ask. You sign on the dotted line and put it out of your mind.

Seven months later (and endless Saturday mornings ruined by the sounds of sledgehammering and power saws) you look out your back window and they've tripled the size of the house. Their "small addition" is now the TRUMP SUNROOM TOWER. There is now a wraparound deck with a bar, built-in seating, two barbecue pits, and a retractable awning that looks like it belongs at the Four Seasons. It's no longer a backyard, it's a resort area. By the time the weather turns warm, strangers begin wandering into the yard. It's like a cruise ship has docked in the neighborhood. In the glow of tiki lamps, people are singing, drinking, and dancing. It's a grand old time for everyone, except those of us who actually live there.

The next time they come asking to add my name to a permit petition, I want to inspect the design, have my own copy of the plans, and reserve the right to veto the project at any point in its development. When I agree to support a small addition to your home, I don't expect to look out my back window weeks later and see a water flume and a monorail.

The CYA Invite

Don't you hate when neighbors you barely know invite you to their big party? The moment you open their email, you know it's a preemptive invite; insurance that you won't call the police when things get out of hand. They actually think a cheesy invitation to their Summer Luau will be enough to keep you from ratting them out to the police when the native drumming and limbo contest is still going strong at 1 a.m. Fat chance.

Occasionally, I'll stop by the parties to check out the spread (to be polite). Then once I get home, I go up to my room, get into my PJs, and call the cops. I figure I already have my alibi! (By the way, the invite doesn't entitle them to overflow parking in my driveway. If their cousin's Subaru is parked there when I come home, I call the tow truck right after I get off the phone with the cops.)

Step Away From the Leaf Blower

A good neighbor does not approach your house with a leaf blower. It is always an act of war. Starting up a leaf blower before 9 a.m. on a Sunday is not acceptable or neighborly. If you don't have a silencer on that thing, grab a broom and sweep quietly.

The leaf-blowing brigade starts early, in hopes of concealing their wrongdoing. Do they think we don't notice when piles of leaves and yard refuse suddenly appear on our front lawns? Do they think we are too dumb to realize that their clippings have migrated onto our driveways? One time, I bagged it all up and deposited it on the front porch of the offending neighbor. Hearing rustling on the porch, he came running to the front door, pulling a robe over his ample frame.

"What are you doing?" he said.

"I'm returning your things. I didn't want you to think that I took them." He stood there shocked, but didn't dare say another word. If you want to blow leaves on someone else's property, on a weekend morning, no less, you'd better be using your lungs.

Reunited . . . and It Doesn't Feel So Good

There is nothing nicer than reconnecting with people you haven't seen in years—and nothing more upsetting than learning that their sudden reemergence has less to do with you than what you can do *for* them. It usually starts with a letter or an email. "Hey, Laura, I was going through some old photos the other day and found this shot of us in New York from 1990. Can you believe we ever wore those shoulder pads?"

Just as the first happy wave of nostalgia begins, you hit the second paragraph, and it dawns on you that this long-lost "friend" is writing for one reason: she wants something from you. The discovered photo was just a convenient pretext to get you to promote her book, endorse a product, share a contact, or write a letter of recommendation for her daughter. Here's a letter of recommendation:

> *Dear ____ :*
>
> *It is so good to hear from you and to see that picture of us after all these years. After reading your letter, I now remember why we lost touch for twenty years. If you're going to ask a favor, it is always best to reestablish the relationship first. To demand a favor after barely making contact with someone would be rude, insensitive, and self-serving. But I'm sure you already knew that. Great to hear from you.*
>
> > *Laura*

Reunions

Let me get this straight . . . I am being asked to clear my schedule and force myself to socialize with people I avoided like the plague in school—and this is supposed to be fun? Does the fact that their faces (and mine) look like they have been squeezed through the Play-Doh Fun Factory change the social math here? If I didn't converse or mingle with these people twenty years ago, why would I want to do so now? Confronting the horrible effects of age and playing "guess the classmate" for four hours is not my idea of a thrilling night out. "Hey, Amanda! Great to see you! Remember that time I was in your room after softball and I was so drunk, my teeth felt numb?" Meanwhile, Amanda has no recollection of either the event or this man standing uncomfortably close to her.

A reunion can go one of two ways: either you discover kind, wonderful people that you didn't meet decades ago (leading to feelings of regret), or you find them to be perfectly horrible (confirming your wisdom in avoiding them in the first place).

I have never attended a college class reunion. Considering that I was under constant assault while editor of the *Dartmouth Review,* and exactly five people rose to my defense—forgive me if I don't join your reunion panel discussion to reminisce about the good old days. When I want to have a reunion, I'll call up my five actual friends from college and invite them out to dinner.

Roomhates

For young people in this economy, roommates are a fact of life—often a miserable one. Getting along with someone you love is hard enough. Getting along with someone you met last week on Craigslist is darn near impossible. In conversations with some of my younger friends, I've determined that today's roommates rarely turn out as advertised.

- *Creepers:* At first, these people seem perfectly normal. They say "good morning" and "good night" and are as polite as can be. Then one day while you are busy getting ready for a date, she stands in the doorway of the bathroom and starts the interrogation. "Where you off to?" This innocent question quickly becomes "Oh, I'm not doing anything tonight. I could get dressed really fast if you want some company." The creeper roommate has begun her advance, insinuating herself into your private business. Any shred of information is used by the creeper for maximum advantage. One of my regular babysitters told her roommate about a big party she was attending and in conversation shared the name of the host. Hours later, after a quick dinner with friends, the girl arrived at the party to find her roommate there. The roommate used the name of the host to get in.

You were looking for someone to offset the rent: now you've acquired a live-in stalker you can't shake. Pretty soon, these creepers are tailing you to movies, the grocery store, lunches, and offering all sorts of input and advice that you never requested and would never use. Make sure to stop the roommate creepers before they start. Tell them nothing except that the rent is due on the twentieth of each month.

- *Neatniks and slobs:* Felix Unger and Oscar Madison are still alive and well. A young woman I know, with a very stressful job, got a text message from her roommate in the middle of the workday. "Don't worry about it," the text read. "I picked up your cereal bowl and spoon. They are in the dishwasher now, where they belong. Cindy." This is the kind of passive-aggressive, neatnik behavior that leads to domestic violence. I have always wondered what the back story was on those crime blotter squibs. Now when I read "Roommate impaled with cereal spoon" I'll know exactly what happened. Hey, roomie, just put the cereal bowl away and keep it to yourself! And the roommate relationship should be terminated altogether the first time a snitty complaint scribbled on a sticky note is left on the fridge.

Then there are the slob roommates. The day before they move in is the last time they appear clean. After that, it's unending days spent with Maury Povich, parked on your sofa, sucking down barrels of Ben & Jerry's. They leave their territorial marks, usually coffee and wine stains on your carpets and upholstery. And even when they are away, their memory lingers via piles of dirty laundry. The biggest challenge: how do you encourage this variety of roommate to vacate? Rather than have an unpleasant discussion with him or go through the hassle of eviction, it might be easier to just report him to the board of health and let the city condemn the place—preferably with the roomie still in it.

- *The Borrowers:* Pity the poor roommate who retrieves her brand-new blouse from the closet, only to discover that it has already been worn. Under the cellophane, the garment looks like it was last used to clean the arena floor at a truck and tractor pull. Does it never occur to the "borrower" roommate that the obvious sweat stains, not to mention the tire tracks, on the clothing might give her away? Apparel isn't the only thing they borrow. These roommates filch food, books, toothpaste, hair spray, and anything else not nailed down. If you find yourself with a borrower in the apartment, direct him to a roommate message board and suggest that he go borrow a new address.

Dog-Eat-Human World

Along with 72 million of my fellow Americans, I own a pet. Dogs have been especially close to my heart ever since 1994, when I met a regal yellow Labrador puppy named Troy. For thirteen years, through career switches, cancer, breakups, and family deaths, we were inseparable. Five years ago, when he escaped from my backyard and went missing for three days, I became distraught and inconsolable. I even absented myself from my radio show and led a multiperson "find Troy" task force in the District of Columbia. It wasn't the most professional thing for me to do when I called into my own show to put out an APB for Troy and began sobbing uncontrollably. Friends who would call me during this search-and-rescue expedition say that they couldn't speak with me for two minutes without my crying out "Troy!" in the most infernal, high-pitched wail.

Lately I've begun to wonder: is there such a thing as loving a pet too much? Are they the new "children" for adults in a state of perpetual adolescence? You know we are no longer "pet owners," we are now "pet parents." There are dogs in baby carriages. Dogs in Halloween costumes. Dogs with their own furniture lines. There's even dog social networking on Dogster and Dogbook. And I know what you're wondering: can dogs and cats really "tweet"? The answer is yes. Twitter is teaming with "pet parents" who want to trade tips and stories about their furry friends.

The American Pet Products Association reports that in 2010, Americans spent a staggering $47.7 billion on their pets. That's exponentially more than is spent across the globe on cancer research. It's true that pets are expensive. I thought my dermatologist's office visits were pricey until I saw what vets get for annual vaccinations. Isn't being rabid part of a dog's nature, after all? And what exactly is in those prescription Frontline and Interceptor pills? They cost eighty bucks for a twelve-pack. Are our dogs ingesting Krugerrands? How did we reach a point where dog food is more expensive than human food? Conservatives recommending cuts to Social Security are often accused of wanting to feed Grandma dog food. Today, the joke no longer makes sense. Have you seen what they charge for a thirty-pound bag of Science Diet? As if Grandma could afford that!

Speaking of eating, since when do our pets need their own bakeries? "Fetch" bakery in Occoquan, Virginia, promises a "new experience in pampering your pet with our gourmet treats"— sixty different "delectable" homemade varieties. (That's all?) It's hard to find moms with the time to make homemade goodies for their *kids* these days, but at least Rover is enjoying his broccoli and sweet potato "brownies."

But dogs can't live on food and medicine alone. They need their proper fluffing and primping. Remember Petey from the Little Rascals? When the "gang" needed to bathe him, they put him in a metal laundry tub and broke out the garden hose. Now Petey would find himself at a place like Artistic Pet Grooming in Broomfield, Colorado. At this "spa for dogs," workers don't call themselves "groomers." "I like to call myself a pet stylist," Melissa Fidge told Denver's ABC News Channel 7. " 'Groomer' has a negative connotation, and I think I take it to the next level." Imagine Petey luxuriating on "hypo-allergenic" pillows, enjoying a "paw-dicure" or a "blueberry facial," as New Age music and nature sounds play in the background. If Petey were too stressed out by Spanky's latest hijinks, he could enjoy the popular "aromatherapy package" (described as "relaxation in a bottle for pets"). Or if the gang were just getting to be too much for Petey, he could grab some downtime abroad at a five-star, luxury pet hotel like the Canis Dog Resort in Germany. For hundreds a day, the stressed pooch can enjoy his own heated dog lodge and lots of pampering from the attentive staff. "Isla, Petey needs more rawhide in lodge number 7A."

Pets are so exalted today that the nomenclature has even changed. In fact, the word "pet" itself is suddenly out of vogue, in favor of the more empathetic term "animal companion." One state assemblyman in California, Nathan Fletcher (R-San Diego), wants to eliminate the term "pound" from state laws and replace it with "animal shelter." He also wants to nix the word "destroy" when used to reference humane euthanasia of an animal. Note that the law is not changing, just the terminology. Assemblyman Fletcher, I know you love your pups, but whether you call it a pound or an animal shelter, it will make no difference to the dog (I mean "animal companion"). Chances are he doesn't understand English. But whatever makes you feel better.

Romance

I know what you're wondering. How does an unmarried woman of a certain age have the nerve to comment on that which she obviously has yet to master? Think of it this way: when you were making that critical decision about your career path or trying to pick a university, you sought the advice of a high school guidance counselor—someone in a dead-end job, making slightly more than the cashier at CVS. I promise you, my experience in this area is more extensive than theirs—that is, unless your life's goal is to be a career counselor to a bunch of smug, pimply-faced teens who all think they are the next Mark Zuckerberg.

Where do I start? From my first boyfriend in summer camp to the cute polo player from a few years back, my observations about the other sex span almost four decades. I am one of those women who have a lot of guy friends. I was a tomboy from the moment I could walk and ripped the heads off Barbie dolls. So it's not a big surprise that when I "grew up," I never was very good at the demure, sweet, and shy act that so many men seem to adore. As you'll see below, I prefer the direct approach.

Check-Mate

Feminists opened doors for women in the workplace, closed doors for babies in the womb, and forced women to start paying their way on dates. The first two are significant; the last is merely annoying. Ladies, don't you hate it when you are out at a nice Italian restaurant with a date, and he doesn't make even the slightest move for his wallet? I mean, not even a feigned reach for the credit card. There's always that awkward moment after the check arrives. Excruciating silence follows. It's like a game of chicken, only it involves who's going to pay for the chicken. Then we're supposed to think he's Prince Charming if he says "Want to split it on two credit cards?" The "splitter" makes the cheapskate Olympics when he justifies paying less than 50 percent of the bill by noting that he didn't order the appetizer or the cosmo, so adjusting his share is equitable. (Ten to one, he's the guy with the tip-calculator app on his phone—not a penny over 15 percent!) And no, the fact that we're in hard economic times doesn't give men a pass, either. If you want to date, maybe it's time to hock that new 55" HD flat-screen you just bought.

Perhaps it's our age-old desire to be protected and provided for, but we ladies are more likely to swoon at the man who refuses to let a woman pay . . . for dinner, a movie, an ice cream cone, anything except maybe his birthday and Christmas gift. The vast majority of women who tell you they are fine going Dutch with a man are lying. My godfather and dear friend, Pat Cipollone, is part of the dying breed of the ever-generous man. A husband and father of ten children, he never in my presence has willingly allowed *anyone* to pick up a check—not even for a Starbucks latte. On the one occasion I sneaked the credit card to the waiter ahead of time to cover the bill, he was extremely unhappy with me. "Don't *ever* do that again," he said. Now *that's* cool.

Cash Flashers

Almost as bad as the perpetual cheapskate is the guy who never stops talking about his money or who shamelessly flaunts it to impress. This is hardly a new phenomenon, but hedge fund billionaires and Silicon Valley mega-moguls have taken the cash flashing up a notch. While on a blind date in Manhattan with a man I was assured was "perfect" for me, I learned he had a yacht, a private jet, a 2,500-bottle wine cellar, and a home in Sun Valley—all before our appetizers had arrived. I think he asked one question of me—"Do you like the wine?" Then he proceeded to tell me it was a Chateau Margaux, and he had just bought six bottles at auction for several thousand dollars. My first thought: what exactly was he compensating for? But you don't have to be wildly rich to be a cash flasher. My friend, a recent college graduate, told me that a forty-something marketing executive approached her and her friends at a bar in Georgetown, not long ago, asking if he could buy their drinks. He pulled out his billfold to reveal exactly one twenty-dollar bill, which he tossed onto the bar, along with his business card. They were supposed to be wowed by his affiliation with a firm they had never heard of, along with President Jackson staring up at them. Oh, and Daddy Warbucks wore a wedding ring.

TMI Syndrome

About ten years ago, I was fixed up with a lawyer (natch) in my area who had been previously married, and was divorced for only six months or so. By the time we got to dessert, I had heard about his ex-wife's affair with an old college pal, what a lousy cook she was, how she didn't understand or care about his practice, and that she routinely forgot to shave her legs. Gee, what a babe magnet he was! Classless. This therapy session couldn't end soon enough.

At the end of the meal, I wanted to look at my watch, fold my arms and say, "I'm afraid that's all the time I have today—let's pick up where we left off next week." At least he paid for dinner.

I Got You, Babe!

Girls—don't you hate it when men call you "babe" or "baby" on the first date? You've known him for less than an hour and he already has a nickname for you! There is nothing worse than faux-coolness and instant familiarity. Of course, there is the distinct possibility that he is calling you "babe" because in his long list of recent conquests, he can't remember your name.

The Texters

Why are people today so loathe to use the telephone to invite someone to a social function? Okay, I can see e-vites for big parties, but if you want to make a statement, don't ask her on a date via text. For example, "U wanna go 2 a mvie Thurs? ;-)" is just not a proposal worth responding to. Clearly he is too lazy, scared, or self-important to pick up the phone to speak with you. And if a man is above the age of sixteen and using emoticons, it's a safe bet that he has some work to do in the maturity department. [:<(

The Waiters

A man should ask you out in person or over the phone. The exception is when he does so on a Friday evening: "So, what are you up to this weekend?" Or "do you want to do something Saturday?" Make a plan, Stan. I was once asked out by a cute polo player who texted, "Why don't we say 8:30 on Saturday and we'll figure out a plan then." This isn't *The Love Boat*, and I'm not Julie McCoy your personal cruise director. We gals like men who call us and say something such as "I have tickets to a show/movie/concert/sporting event that I think you'll really like, and will pick you up at eight. Does that work for you?" It exudes confidence and strength.

Showing Him the Door

Then there are the men who don't walk you to the door at the end of a date. Where did they learn this? My (now) friend J. was notorious for doing this until I offered a little friendly correction. One night, I swear, he barely slowed down. Finally, I'd had it. Once out of the car, I yelled down the street, "Hey J., you forgot something!!" Hearing me, he backed up. "What did I forget?" he asked. "The tire tracks you left on the street when you burned rubber just now!" Why bother stopping at all? Just slow down to 15 mph and have me do a combat roll into the street!

Drop-Dead Lines

One of the many annoyances of single life is having to suffer through the ridiculous icebreakers men intone to strange women. They are known as pickup lines, but I've always referred to them as drop-dead lines—any man using them is already dead to me. Here is but a small sampling of the choice lines I have heard, but wish I hadn't:

- "Do you have any Band-Aids, because I just skinned my knees falling for you?"
- "Are you a parking ticket? Because you've got fine written all over you."
- "I hope you're a nurse, because I might need oxygen. You take my breath away."
- "Do you have a map, because I keep getting lost in your eyes?"
- "I'm kind of sleepy. Is your place nearby?"
- "Your body must be Visa because it's everywhere I want to be."
- "I may not be the best-looking guy in here, but I'm the only one talking to you."

Gents, if you ever want to have a relationship with a woman not confined to your iPad, drop the pickup lines. They make you seem creepy, juvenile, and worse, unimaginative. If you want a decent woman's attention, a simple "hello" will do. First impressions matter, and once you utter a drop-dead line, the impression of you is set. That's right, you're a loser.

Wedding Planning

I write this knowing full well the impending blowback. "As a single woman, how dare she comment on something she's never experienced?" Fair criticism, unless you consider that I've come close to the altar twice, and the most recent occasion gave me some perspective on today's wedding mania. During the four weeks or so back in 2005 that I was engaged, I was afforded a telling glimpse into a world that I had previously only viewed from afar. To me, it felt like the first time I watched *Mutual of Omaha's Wild Kingdom* as a kid and saw the exotic snakes of the Amazon. Except I actually enjoyed watching an anaconda hunt its prey with "Jim" huddled behind a nearby tree. I felt no such fascination flipping through the bridal magazines that a concerned friend dropped off at my studio. What is wrong with me, I wondered?

My friend Melinda was both shocked and amused at how un-bridelike I seemed. "Maybe you should hire a 'wedding planner,'" she suggested. "You don't have the time or patience to put on a wedding," she said. She was right, I didn't. But who knew how much time it took to interview wedding planners?

One extremely successful (and expensive) wedding consultant arrived at my house with a "portfolio" of her work. (Of course, I immediately wondered what type of couple would agree to have

the details of their blessed union used in promotional materials.)
"Who are you, Frank Gehry?" I joked. With a straight face she
shot back, "In a manner of speaking, yes. I am the architect of the
perfect wedding. I build dreams." That was a short meeting.

Due to the somewhat public nature of my ill-fated engage-
ment, the wedding industry was knocking at my door at every
turn—but I didn't answer. Invitations had to be ordered. Entrees
had to be selected. Guest lists had to be finalized. But I was
aggressively annoyed and bored by it all. Today the business of
wedding planning is even bigger. One popular website called
the Knot (www.theknot.com) brags that members will have
"exclusive access" to photos of twenty thousand wedding gowns.
One could be celebrating her silver anniversary and still not have
reviewed that number! If I had to rate which was more enjoyable,
trying on wedding dresses or undergoing chemotherapy, it would
be a toss-up.

When one of the wedding planners I auditioned asked if I had
"settled on a videographer," I replied, "No, in fact, I don't think I
really want to video the wedding." By the expression on her face,
you might have thought I had told her the wedding ceremony
would feature a satanic sacrifice. "Well, I assume you know that
these days it's not a question of whether you hire a videographer,
but how many." Yes, it's true, I was behind the curve. Multicam-
era shoots are all the rage now, complete with cutaway interviews
with wedding guests and original score compositions to make a
couple's big day truly worthy of remembering. Just what I en-

visioned lurking among the pews during my wedding Mass: a wannabe James Cameron leading the team that shot *Titanic*.

Then there were the headsets. Another hot matrimonial facilitator took a little Secret Service–type earpiece out of her purse at our first meeting and said, "This ensures that I'll be able to handle any last-minute contingency and communicate with my entire team during the process." The "process"? How romantic. The "team"? Now the wedding had morphed into my own mini-WPA! And the headset—I kept thinking Janet Jackson circa her "Rhythm Nation" tour.

By the time I met with the "floral designers" in town, I was so over it. "What exactly makes your centerpieces any better than the typical 'spring mix' bouquet I can buy at Safeway for fourteen ninety-nine?" I asked one very intense forty-something "rose artisan" (only half jokingly). "I don't think we have complementary visions," she snapped back. Guess her roses weren't dethorned.

The Bridegroom Is on Life Support

The twenty-year-old marrying the octogenarian can always be relied on to say "age doesn't matter." But when the old coot asks for a Huggie and she reaches for the overnights with the no-leak design, age matters!

To defend their May-December nuptials, they'll inevitably say, "We're marrying for love." Oh, stop. He may be marrying for love, but you are marrying for money. I'm sure there are a few exceptions, but let's be honest; if gramps were gumming his Jell-O in a retirement home and not as lord of the Playboy Mansion, I doubt if any of these women would give him the time of day.

Speaking of Hugh Hefner . . . the eighty-five-year-old recently announced his intention to marry twenty-four-year-old Crystal Harris. Claiming that the age gap was irrelevant, Hef's fiancée told CNN's Piers Morgan (Cue the "Lie of the Day" music), "I have so much fun with him. It's hard for me to keep up with him." The only people who can't keep up with Hefner these days are infants and the handicapped.

For his part, the old letch got all romantic about the union: "Age really is just a number. You don't know how long you've got; how long's an average marriage last?" Apparently, longer than your decency, pal. But what we can infer from Hefner's statement is that at least he realizes this will be his last visit to church outside a casket, and that Crystal has most assuredly signed the prenup.

There are a few ways to discern whether the groom is too old for the bride. For instance: If the preferred wedding presents are Polident gift packs, you know the groom is too old for the bride. If the bride's parents could be the groom's grandchildren, you know he is too old for the bride. If the groom's heirs start to pray before the vows that the new Mr. and Mrs. have no offspring, you know the groom is too old for the bride. When the groom's daughters are the bridesmaids, and four decrepit women lead the bride down the aisle, you know the groom is too old for the bride.

I have met women who say their (much) older husbands give them a sense of security that they could not enjoy with a younger spouse. One friend told me that she is less concerned about aging because he's "already so old." Using that logic, we should all revel in our youth and go out and marry a cadaver. When an eighty-two-year-old is marrying a girl who is a fourth of his age, can we admit there is a problem? You don't have a father figure complex, sweetie, you have a great-grandfather complex!

The Garter Belt Tradition

This dates back to the fourteenth century, when it was thought to be good luck to obtain a part of a bride's wedding dress. As you can imagine, this meant a lot of wedding gowns were ripped to shreds, so by necessity, the tradition gradually evolved. Women began wearing separate garters to give away. Wikipedia tells us, "It is the groom's privilege to remove the garter and toss it to the male guests. The symbolism to deflowering is unambiguous." Here's an idea—let's limit the tradition to those women who actually have yet to be deflowered!

I was twelve years old, attending my first wedding, when I witnessed the garter belt interlude. It was traumatic. Seeing the groom snake his hands up a big pile of wedding gown material, then use his teeth to drag the garter down his bride's leg as invited guests whooped and hollered, I thought, my parents are letting me watch this?

Almost as bad as the garter belt ceremony is the music chosen to accompany it. Some recent classics (posted on YouTube!): "Hot in Here" by Nelly; "Girls" by the Beastie Boys; "Legs" by ZZ Top; and "Sweet Cherry Pie" by Warrant. Of course, the worst is when the groom actually sings a karaoke version of the above to the guests while shimmying up his beloved's thigh.

Some websites offer "garter belt joke" ideas—where a bride and groom collude to tie bizarre items to the garter belt such as a rubber chicken, a toaster, a yo-yo, or the very subtle banana. Ehow.com recommends: "When it is time for the garter toss, have the groom take the smaller items out from the garter first. Be sure to have him hold the item up to the audience so that they may see what he is pulling out as well as the confused look on his face." Since when did wedding receptions become a night at the Ha Ha Hut?

Do-It-Yourself Vows

Don't you hate weddings where the bride and groom drop the word "obey" from their vows—or worse, write their own? Unless you're Edna St. Vincent Millay, spare us the original composi-tions and stick with the traditional text. And that goes for you, Duke and Duchess of Canterbury!

They usually write something like: "I promise to celebrate you and our love all the days of my life . . ." You can almost hear the "unless you get very ill or I get a better offer" disclaimer. If you are going to subject us to meaningless vows like this, why don't you two just keep dating, and I'll hold on to this Vitamix blender?

Congratulations—You're the Photographer

Don't you love it when you arrive at your table at the wedding reception and each chair has a disposable camera on it? Were they expecting Annie Leibovitz? Why am I forced into playing photographer for the event? I'm a guest, not unpaid staff.

They would never leave fabric and thread on the seat and expect us to embroider the honeymoon outfits, but modern wedding planners think we should all pitch in and fill their book of memories. Inevitably, only the most plastered guests end up snapping photos. These reception photos turn out looking like stills from *The Blair Witch Project*. Like the cameras that captured them, they are truly disposable. Hey, Mr. and Mrs. Whoever, if you want candid shots of the guests at your wedding, hire a second photographer.

Videotaping the Wedding

It is one thing to video your wedding. It is quite another thing to turn it into an IMAX experience. Here's a tip: if there is a production truck in front of the church and a floor director on the altar, you have gone too far with the wedding video. I attended one wedding where the "director" actually warmed up the congregation and coached us on when we should clap. I was waiting for a blinking applause sign to lower from the ceiling.

Then once they get the masterpiece edited, the couple has a party where they "premiere" the video. You know, some things are best left to memory. If the wedding video is really overproduced, there'll be lots of cheesy close-ups of the bride and groom interspersed with slow-mo shots of them dancing. But the true sign that your wedding video is completely over the top is when it includes a montage of well wishes from the attendees. I thought I agreed to be a guest at your wedding, not a participant in the latest episode of *Bridezillas.*

5

Skhool 4 Foolz

Today we obsess more than ever about our children's education. Parents move their families to avoid bad schools and to be closer to good ones. They hire tutors to help their offspring learn the alphabet and take the ACT. They stay up until all hours doing their kids' physics project. But are our children smarter and more well-adjusted than they were thirty years ago? Don't answer until you finish this chapter.

Today parents aggressively jockey to get their children spots in fancy preschools, grammar schools, and high schools. And they're starting earlier than ever before. "I just dropped off Eva's application for Crossroads Academy," a chic young mother recently confided to me at a dinner party. "I figured I'd better start early if she's going to get into Brown!" I was dying to say "Hey, lady, Eva hasn't even been conceived yet, so chill!"

Yet being a mom myself, I can relate. It's not easy out there. Just reading report cards these days requires an advanced degree in hieroglyphics. Then there are the moral dilemmas: Should I order her the hot lunch or brown-bag it? Buy all of the chocolate bars for the school's fall candy sale, or stand outside Target on Saturday to unload them myself? Should I let him get the C grade in science, or just build the fully functioning water treatment facility for him in my free time? It all begs the question: How after twenty years of hard work and struggle did I end up where I began: begging for grades, sweating projects, and cramming? The good news is, graduation does come eventually: when the kids get married and move out of your house.

Redshirting Kindergarteners

In the 1970s, when I grew up, children who were held back a year were—to put it charitably—academically, and often behaviorally, challenged. This was usually the decision of school officials, not parents. Only children born after October 1 of their kindergarten year were eligible to be held back. It was unheard of for a child born in, say, June (yours truly) or March (!!), to be held back by parents on maturity or developmental grounds. Not so today, where parents hold kids back in school like security guards hold back fans at a Lady Gaga concert. Redshirting is all the rage for parents who want to give their children (especially boys) an "edge" in academics or sports. It's just what you do if your little one has a birthday that falls in April or beyond.

In Texas, these are called "Primer" grades. A close friend whose children attended Highland Park Presbyterian in Dallas tells me that it is not uncommon for a boy to be held back in Kindergarten because his sixth birthday fell in February! This causes a startlingly skewed dynamic in the student's later years. Kim volunteers at the cafeteria in her child's school. She reports that in seventh grade, where the students should be twelve years old, many of the "boys" are already shaving. "They come through the lunch line and they look like freshmen in college. I have to remind myself that they're not even freshmen in high school yet!" The fourteen-year-old redshirts are a full foot taller than the boys whose parents didn't obsess about giving them the leg up in lacrosse or football.

Query: Why hold kids back for only one year? Why not three? Soon elementary school graduation will look like the Notre Dame commencement!

Kindergarten Tutors

Expectations are so high for a child entering first grade that teachers are increasingly recommending that parents hire tutors to "fill the knowledge gaps." Excuse me, isn't that *your* job? I know a whole cadre of people who have now submitted their kindergartners to intensive outside instruction. These tutors charge up to eighty dollars an hour. At those prices, I hope they're teaching the kids Greek and Mandarin—and flying them to Mykonos and Beijing. What happened to the joys of being five, when the focus of your "study" was creating macaroni art and knowing the colors of the rainbow? I have an idea—maybe we should get the teachers tutors so we can fill their "knowledge gaps."

Class Screenings

Over dinner one night, a friend asked her daughter what she did at school that day. She expected the child to tell her about the new words she had learned, or the country she had studied. Instead the girl told her mother, "We watched *The Little Mermaid* today." Well, I guess Louis singing "Les Poissons" is one way to learn French.

When I consulted friends, some of whom live in other states, they revealed that their children also watched movies routinely during the school day. We don't send kids to school to watch movies they already own. These screenings are eating away precious class time when they should be learning something substantive; not zoning out in front of a cartoon so the teacher can take a break. Entertainment has intruded on so many aspects of our lives, surely the school should be a safe zone. We want our kids to be able to add and to spell—they can learn SpongeBob jingles at home. The school experience should feel more like *The Paper Chase* and less like *Glee*. If this now passes for education, maybe we should divert our tuition dollars toward Netflix gift cards and let the kids sleep in.

Young Teacher, Old Teacher

There are basically three varieties of teachers: seasoned veterans who know the score, greenhorns too inexperienced to know that they shouldn't have taken the position in the first place, and those who are looking ahead for the next job.

- *The Old-Timers:* Easily recognized, these educators are surprised by nothing in the classroom, betray little emotion, and always let the kids know who owns the class. Don't try any games with these vets. Rules are clearly spelled out at the first bell, and those who violate them suffer immediate chastisement, punishment, or both. Experienced teachers know how to impose their will on thirty kids and keep them in check. Malefactors are given demerits, placed in a seat of shame (usually red), or sent to the stockades—not necessarily in that order. What I like about these tried-and-true vets is that they are there to teach students, not befriend or coddle them. They also don't let parents sweet-talk them into giving the kids a pass. After all, they probably taught these fast-talking parents at one time, as well. Some common characteristics: a low, stern voice; a ruler, stick, or other instrument of coercion firmly in hand at all times; eyes capable of shooting daggers; and a classroom demeanor reminiscent of General Patton or Judge Judy. By the way, I love these teachers.

- *The Newbies:* These are the overly eager, bright-eyed young teachers who bound about trying to impress students the way a puppy tries to impress the couple that just walked into the pound. Children have a name for these untested teachers: victims. The pitiful neophytes live by their teaching plan as if it were a new gospel. Every movement in the day is choreographed like a Russian military parade. The façade of efficiency begins to crumble at the first crisis. The minute little Suzy sticks a pencil in Johnny's right eye during "centers," the newbie teacher goes into a panic. There are no lesson plans that include blood-splattered Legos. This is when you need a grizzled warhorse, not a trembling recent college grad.

- *The "Transition" Teacher:* These are real doozies. They've been at the school for seven to ten years, and still consider the job a mere "stepping stone" to his or her *real* career. Parent–teacher conferences with these "educators" usually end with this closer: "You know, I worked at my college radio station. Any advice for someone who wants to get into the business?"

My advice, go with the old-timers. They know their stuff and won't take any guff from petulant students or their pampered parents. And they're not looking for the next job. They have the novel idea that when you master a profession you love, you keep at it.

Dumb Days

In addition to the school-created holidays ("teacher planning days," "parent–teacher conference days"), there are an array of other specialty days that should be struck from the academic calendar. I refer to the string of faux homeroom holidays that have proliferated at elementary schools in recent years:

- *Backwards Day:* This day is particularly distressing: For seven hours your child is compelled to wear his or her clothes inside out and wrong way round. When the final bell rings, they look like escapees from a lunatic asylum. Why would we teach children to dress improperly? It's hard enough getting them to put the clothes on the right way. Though, maybe I'm being too harsh. What parent wouldn't relish sending their child off in the morning with a hearty "Have a great day, sweetheart—you look like an insane homeless person."

- *Pajama Day:* A chance for your child to frolic through the dirty halls of school in their sleep clothes. If you happen to wear footie pajamas, it's not so bad. But for little girls with flimsy nightgowns this is a hygienic nightmare. Pajamas were meant to sleep in, not as optional outerwear. It's no wonder that we see college students now wearing pajamas on planes and adults wearing pajamas to the gym—they picked up the fashion alternative in elementary school. If we're going to wear inappropriate fashions at school, why not institute Swimwear Day, Animal Hides Day, or Thong Day? Then again, maybe Pajama Day is just an example of administrators being practical. If the kids are going to sleep in class, they may as well be comfortable.

- *Jeans Day:* Some of us chose certain schools based on their policy of student uniforms. It's nice not having to worry about impressing classmates with your couture. But on Jeans Day, students are encouraged to dress like slobs and wear jeans to school. Worse, some schools demand that the child pay for the privilege. So let me get this straight: I pay a steep tuition so that my child can wear a uniform, then I buy the overpriced ensemble from the only authorized dealer, only to have the school later intimidate me into paying three bucks so my child can wear overpriced jeans. I give up.

- *Crazy Hair Day:* On these days kids can style their hair any way they choose. It typically involves lots of hair gel and color spray. But given the state of kids' grooming recently, it's hard to tell the difference between Crazy Hair Day and Everyday Hair Day.

Yearbooks

Haven't we had it with grammar school yearbooks? If I want a publication filled with pictures of other people's children, I'll buy a copy of *American Girl* magazine. The schools now make you pre-order the books, so no matter what's inside, you can't return it.

Flipping through the yearbook (once you finally get it, usually a year later) is like playing the school edition of Where's Waldo. For $20, you scour each page hoping to find a stray shot of your child. If you're lucky, there's a grainy shot of a part of your kid's body, obstructed by some other child:

"There's my daughter's hair at the class picnic."

"There's the back of her head on the swing."

"Oh, there she is playing chase in the school yard. She's the blur there on the left."

Face it, the only sure shots of your kid is the official individual portrait, which is always a dicey affair. For whatever reason, most kids look like they were just woken up by the paparazzi. Other poor children appear to be posing for mug shots at central lockup. The teachers must take a powder during the photo session, because all the kids have bows, collars, and glasses that are either askew or falling off. The group picture is just as bad. The photographer always seems to capture the children just as their expressions are fading. But the teacher always looks good.

Truth is, the only kids who look great and are regularly featured throughout the yearbook are the children of PTA members, and those who chronically volunteer for every school activity.

Project Planners—and Doers

When a third grader comes into class carrying a homemade telescope outfitted with internal HD camera capability and laser crosshairs, do we really believe that the kid built it himself? Scores of elementary school teachers now assign projects that are so involved and elaborate that they have, by necessity, become parental undertakings.

I remember going to school with a sagging piece of poster board bearing hand-drawn sketches of the solar system with some scrawl beneath the planets. Today, kids are expected to build a fully functional nuclear reactor and demonstrate some fission events for the class. Okay, I might be exaggerating a little, but when the science fair starts to look like the Northrop Grumman showroom, there is no way children are constructing these projects themselves. Can we get back to building baking soda volcanoes?

At his school, my friend Rebecca's son was assigned an International Day project. He had to prepare a report on a chosen country (Poland), bring in authentic food, and create a native costume for an in-class presentation. (Why not just make the kid fly to Krakow?) Rebecca had her son research and write his report, hot-glue a costume from old clothes around the house, and helped him whip up some pierogi. When presentation day rolled around, she and her son felt like refugees who had been denied access to Ellis Island. In the school gym, a child who had done his project on Italy drove in on a Vespa scooter. He handed out cannolis while dressed as the Pope. A girl, who picked France for her assignment, wore a can-can outfit. Her parents, in French waiter costumes, served quiche Lorraine to the assembled. Not only should these parents have been embarrassed, they should have been deported! If parents are going to do their children's work, they should forgo the charade and just put their names on the projects. Why let Junior suck up all your glory? Go and get that first-place ribbon and wear it with pride. After all, *you* earned it!

Wrapping Paper and Chocolate

I understand that schools need to raise money to balance their budgets, but do they have to turn our kids into door-to-door salesmen to do it? Every year, I dread the arrival of the chocolate boxes or wrapping paper order forms. Are these the only products they could come up with to push on the relatives? When did chocolate and wrapping paper become such sought-after products? How about offering some innovative, practical home and garden items that we can actually use? Instead, my kid is spending the afternoon trying to sell large quantities of things you can find in the checkout aisle at Target.

Frankly, I don't want to buy wrapping paper at these exorbitant prices. That's what God made dollar stores for. And the wrapping paper that schools offer is always thick and metallic—like colored aluminum foil. I guess if you don't have anyone on your gift list, you can always use it to tent your Christmas ham.

Still, like most parents, I feel bad, so I bully friends and family into buying rolls of the stuff. Then, in a show of solidarity, I buy a few twenty-five-dollar rolls myself. I currently have a closet full of wrapping paper. I don't give gifts anymore—at these prices, I just send out wrapping paper.

As bad as the gift wrap is, it's safer than the chocolate. That off-brand stuff that these kids hawk tastes like it was left over from the former Soviet Union. The bars of chocolate are always at least a year old (check the expiration date!) and broken into little pieces. Any time you open a chocolate wrapper and the bar is starting to turn white, you know it either washed ashore or was part of a school sale.

Rather than sending them out to push inferior products on street corners, schools should be encouraging students to study. Or is this vocational training for the only job they'll be able to secure in the Obama economy: selling overpriced foodstuffs and paper products to the neighbors?

The Land of Endless Auctions and Galas

There are some annual school events that I think we could all do without. Chief among them: the school auction and gala. As parents, we are not only guilted into attending these functions, but we have to pay to get in. It's one thing to pay for a good meal, fantastic entertainment, and even great company. But what happens when you get cold chicken, an off-key children's choir, and a chair next to a urologist? And why are we wearing black ties and gowns to go to the school gym?!

Auctions are even more offensive. Months before the event, you get a mailer shaking you down for items to donate. They're always worded thusly: "We know we can count on you to support your child and the mission of Happydale School. Some families in (your child)'s class have already donated: vacations homes, rare wines, romantic dinner packages, and signed precious collectibles. What can we expect from you? All items will be displayed by class on a dedicated table at the auction." After reading one of these extortion letters, you feel as though you should be donating your primary residence or maybe a lung, just to keep up with the other families.

Then when the big night finally arrives, and after you pay $100 to wander about the cafeteria to gawk at tables of gift baskets and luxurious goodies, you make a terrible discovery. No one is bidding on your "Dinner Cruise Along the Potomac with two violinists from the Kennedy Center" package. Out of shame, you place a high bid on your own item, which you later win by default. School auctions are basically opportunities for you to donate items that you will later purchase from the school at a higher price (only after you pay them admission). Next time, I'll just write the school a big check and save myself the trouble and the gown.

Student Evaluations

Elementary school report cards should come with their own decoder rings. The younger the child, the more impossible it is for the parent to decipher how they are doing in class. Gone are the A, B, C, D, and "you are locked in your room until your wedding" grades of the past. Now each report card has its own code and inscrutable acronyms. As the child progresses, these acronyms change and morph into even more confusing arrangements. One kindergarten report card offered these classifications of educational achievement: "C" and "I." When I first saw the row of "C's" and "I's" on the card, I thought, "Does that stand for 'Crummy and Ineffectual'?" The grade "C" (according to the minuscule key that is invisible to the naked eye) means "Consistently Demonstrates." The grade "I" (according to the same key viewed under a microscope) means "Inconsistently Demonstrates." But depending on what the child is "demonstrating," this could be a positive or a negative. For instance, if the kindergartner is "Consistently Demonstrating" self-control, that is wonderful. But if he is "Consistently Demonstrating" a need to nap because he finds the course of study unchallenging, this could be a problem.

A first-grade report card, from a public school, grants scores based on a student's "effort"—not their achievement, but their effort. Making heads or tails of the "effort" grades are just as vexing as the "C, I" report card. Effort indicators include: O for Outstanding, S for Satisfactory, and N for Needs Improvement.

The report card I saw had lots of O's and S's and a few M's. Turns out M indicates "Meets Standard" and is a "Progress Indicator." So let me try to understand this: the teacher grades the child's effort in a given area, but if they have shown no discernible effort, the kid's "progress" is then evaluated. If you are confused, don't dare ask the teacher to clarify it for you.

The fact is that the teacher doesn't understand the evaluation marks, either—she didn't create the system. But as an employee of the school, she's got to put something in the report cards at the end of the quarter, and so long as the S's and O's line up, what the hey? Ask her to explain the standard by which the grades are awarded and she is likely to offer evasive answers or drop your kid's "cooperation with others" score next quarter. I have seen parents argue with teachers over the C's and I's, O's and S's, trying to prove that they deserve a higher grade. Let me help you here—if your children listen and don't cause too much trouble they are Outstanding (O) or Satisfactory (S), but if they are back-talking troublemakers, don't be surprised if they are wrapped in a string of Needs Improvements (N) at the end of the quarter. Personally, I think the whole report card system needs improvement (N) and standardization. Teachers need to Get A Backbone (GAB) and honestly evaluate student performance, while parents need to stop bullying instructors for grades and Accept The Truth (ATT) about their kids' rotten performance.

Everybody Wins

Last year I attended a neighborhood child's final soccer game of the season. The little boy played his heart out and scored three goals during the game. The boy clearly outperformed everyone on the field. After the game, as the kids downed punch and Cheetos, the coach presented the awards. The little boy was thrilled when his name was called. He leapt forward to claim the brass trophy topped by a spinning soccer ball. He hugged his mother and high-fived his dad. Then the coach called the name of every other child on the team, giving each one the exact same award. The little boy threw his trophy on the ground and asked his mother if they could leave.

It has become routine for schools to confer awards on everyone. Now, this may build self-esteem, but it also renders the awards meaningless. Some schools do the same thing at field days. After competing, all the kids receive awards for "participating." Unless you are deployed by the U.S. military, you should not receive a medal for just showing up. This is a deeply unfair practice, because it negates achievement and extinguishes initiative. It sends the message that no matter what you do, the outcome is the same. The kid who sits on the sidelines playing his Nintendo DS will get the same award as the kid hustling to make the goal. It is an atrocious life lesson for young people. Wait until they try to get into college—we'll see how that approach works out for them.

Grammarians at the Gate

I have read the writing of scads of recent college graduates. They often send me letters seeking employment, copies of articles from college papers, etc. One thing emerges from my encounters with their writing: somehow, they managed to get through seventeen years of education without learning the difference between "there" and "their." (For the record, "there" indicates place. "Their" indicates possession.) The grammatical slips among college grads (and too many of their elders) are legion and now widely accepted.

So I take it upon myself to inform them that "loose" and "lose" are not interchangeable. Neither are "your" and "you're" (one indicates possession, and the other is a contraction for "you are"). With apologies to Justice Sonia Sotomayor, "imminent" and "eminent" are also not equivalent. And don't even get me started on "its" and "it's."

Speaking to these college grads is even more distressing than reading their drivel. "Me and Harry just got back from the Hill . . ." No, no, no. "Me and Harry," despite the common usage by certain politicians and their wives, is always incorrect. It can only be "Harry and I." Period. I'm considering making Strunk & White mandatory reading for anyone seeking employment, or even visiting my office. If perchance any of these grammatical slipups make their way into the copy of this book, it's the copy-editor's fault.

Dirty Dancing Is Tame

Young people have, for several decades, danced in a suggestive manner. The Twist, the Bump, and countless other dances were considered risqué in their time. But what happens when suggestive dances turn explicit?

A friend who recently chaperoned a high school dance reported that students were "dry humping" each other all over the dance floor. "It wasn't just a few of them . . . and the girls had next to nothing on," he said. "When I stepped in to break up some of the real offensive stuff, I felt like I was intruding on something intimate."

The kids call this style of dancing (I use the term lightly) "grinding" or "freaking." I have personally witnessed one of these syncopated sex acts at a wedding reception when a group of young people took to the floor and basically writhed all over each other. As I recall, I grabbed a piece of cake and headed for the door. Ingraham Rule of Thumb: if you can get an STD doing it, it's probably not a dance.

In school gyms and cafeterias across the country, the prom now looks like the grotto at Hef's mansion. School district officials are attempting to deal with the dirty dancing epidemic in creative ways. Brighton High school outside of Detroit recently required students to sign a contract (vowing to keep their pelvises to themselves) if they wanted to attend the school dance, and promised to remove anyone caught "freaking" or "grinding." Fifteen hundred students were expected to attend. Only sixty-seven showed up. A high school in Oregon also outlawed "freaking" and offered the kids real dance classes before the prom. Students rioted. That's what happens when kids are exposed to explicit material for years on television and at the Cineplex. They consider the lewd antics of their favorite performer as completely acceptable and something to be replicated.

While school districts and concerned parents are trying to rein in the trashy dancing, First Lady Michelle Obama is leading the young in the opposite direction. Under the auspices of her "Let's Move" initiative, Obama recruited the rump-shaking, flesh-bearing Beyoncé to help her launch a national dance demonstration at more than six hundred middle schools across the country. Reworking her song "Get Me Bodied" ("Bodied" is slang for "freak" dancing), Beyoncé shot a new video featuring herself grooving in stilettos and denim short shorts in a cafeteria full of students. The video was then distributed to middle schools in April of 2011. For weeks young children were taught to bump and grind, strut and suggestively spread their legs just like Beyoncé. Then on May 3, 2011, Michelle Obama led the national "dance-in"—a chance for children, at taxpayer expense, to emulate a sexed-up singer and perform her raunchy dance moves during the school day. Rack up another great accomplishment for Michelle Obama. She can now relabel her initiative as "Let's Move . . . Away From Decency."

Stripper routines and grinding genitalia to musical accompaniment are not dancing, kids—I don't care how many calories you burn at school. If that's your idea of a dance at the prom, tell Mommy to save money on a corsage and just get you a motel room.

Coarse College Courses

A new study recently revealed that nearly half of college students learn next to nothing in their freshman and sophomore years. Maybe it's because they're majoring in binge drinking and ultimate Frisbee. Or maybe there are other contributing factors ...

The porn industry has started offering free screeners of its product to colleges in an effort to lure in young customers. Digital Playground, a smut studio in L.A., made headlines when the University of Maryland scheduled a showing of one of their porn flicks. When state senators protested a publicly funded university's offering this kind of fare, the ACLU and a few loony professors showed the porn anyway—describing it as a "Teach-In." *Time* magazine reports that English professor Martha Nell Smith argued that "literature from Shakespeare to Dickinson includes pornographic elements." Students choose to study erotica, she said, and "our job together is to contextualize it." Contextualize this: you're not a professor—you're lazy, and you're a porn addict. Get help!

Maybe it's time to wrap these whacked-out professors and their coarse offerings in a big brown paper wrapper, complete with a parental warning: "Major in Smut: Only $45K a Year."

6

Disgracebook ;-)

If you have "friends" whom you have never laid eyes on or shared oxygen with, chances are you are living in a technology cocoon. Today there are millions of people living within these self-constructed bubbles. For them, social interaction is posting a grammatically questionable opinion on a message board or join-ing an online group dedicated to a common pursuit. How about pursuing that little thing called life? Take a walk and interact with real people for a change.

These cocooners have mastered the art of independent to-getherness. They occupy the same space as others, but adamantly refuse to engage the environment surrounding them. Bopping to their iPods, with their pupils fixed on laptop screens, they are oblivious to the world around them. They are constantly "connected" but disconnected from the people and things that matter most. The frequency and intensity with which they monitor their incoming texts would lead you to believe that they had the overnight shift at NORAD. But they're really just cocooners who take up space at Starbucks all day, updating their Facebook profiles and Twitter pages, their earbuds plugged into a mystery device.

Maybe you know someone like this and want to bust him out of this unnatural environment for a real social encounter—maybe dinner or drinks. Good luck. Socializing with a cocooner can be like eating with a member of that Amazonian tribe you saw featured last night on National Geographic Channel. Actually, that's underestimating the tribesmen's capacity for human interaction. Since cocooners spend half the evening eyeing their cell phones, you start to feel as if there were three of you at the table. You spy him tapping out messages underneath the table while he pretends to be listening to what you're saying. "Uh-huh . . . wow . . . cool." With half his limited mental abilities devoted to his digital companion, these are the only comments he can make. Problem is, you just told him that your dad died three weeks ago of lung cancer.

Too many of those who grew up in the technology cocoon can text at the speed of light, but they are losing the ability to read verbal and physical cues. This should not be surprising. When you spend more time gazing at your iPad than into the eyes of another human being, what do you expect?

Cocooners socialize on computers, watch entertainment on

computers, listen to music on computers, take pictures with computers, and generally experience all of life through devices big and small. We have spawned an entire generation of tech zombies, people for whom Facebook, Second Life, texting, and Web surfing have supplanted real life. Never in human history have so many replaced so much with so little.

Tech Campers

One afternoon last March, I was rushing up the sidewalk in Georgetown—I had exactly one hour to find and buy a pair of black sandals for a dinner I was going to that night. When I turned the corner, I walked right into a two-man tent set up on the side of the street. I broke my fall atop a Coleman stove. "Hey, watch it, lady!" a college kid screamed out. Glancing to my left, I thought, "What the—?" Down the block a stream of humanity surrounded itself with sleeping bags and grills. The line snaked down the street and around the corner, and the atmosphere was festival-like. I passed at least one mime, two jugglers, and a group of teens playing hacky sack. This was not a line to give blood for some mass disaster, it was a line to buy the new Apple iPad 2.

"How long have you been camping out like this?" I asked a fellow wearing a brown knit cap that looked like it had been worn at the original Woodstock Festival. "Only three days," he muttered. "The last Star Wars movie was way worse—that was four days and no Porta-John."

Walk in front of the Apple Store on a "release day" and you'd swear these people were going to war in Afghanistan. They've got pup tents, portable coolers, solar-powered televisions, and fridges. All for a gadget that will be obsolete minutes after purchase. And why, pray tell, must they have it on the first day? Did Apple manufacture only three of these "must-have" devices?

It's what I call "tech vanity" that drives these campers out of their homes and onto the curb of the Best Buy. After they nab one, they spend the rest of their afternoon making random visits to coffee shops and stores to show off their new wares. Their preferred targets: those poor slobs who have the previous generation of the tech device they just landed.

"Oh, you have the *old* iPad?" the tech camper says to the sucker sitting with his 2009 model at the next table. "Well, I guess you don't really need the iPad 2, unless having a smaller, faster tablet—with two cameras—is important to you."

Laptop People

They hole up in coffee shops and cafés for hours at a time. If you look closely, you can find them: the laptop people (LP). These are the folks who turn public spaces into their own personal offices. The laptop gang spans all age groups, but its members share a few distinguishing characteristics:

- The laptop is always up. This defensive barrier discourages interaction, and obscures the fact that the LP is pathetically sitting alone.

- Papers, pens, day planners, books, and refreshments are scattered about. This gives the appearance of productivity, even though they are just playing Texas Hold 'Em.
- LPs are known for their intense facial expressions. This conceals the brutal facts: that they are unemployed, lonely, and reading the Daily Kos.

None of this is meant as an attack on the LPs. By and large, they are a nonthreatening group who, assuming regulated caffeine intake, will simply stare at their screens for a few hours and go on their way. I write with some authority on this subject, as I myself am a recovering LP. I am happy to report that it has been a year, three months, fourteen days, sixteen hours, twenty minutes and seven seconds since I last opened my laptop in a public place. One day at a time.

In-Your-Facebook

High school reunions usually happen every five to ten years and last a few hours, but on Facebook, it's like you're trapped at a reunion forever. Out of the kindness of your heart, or maybe out of mild curiosity, you "friended" people whom you never wanted as actual friends in the first place. Facebook has become a forum to complain, share TMI, air dirty laundry and other inane thoughts all day long. It's a colossal time-suck; a way for students and adults to avoid living. What is it about people who feel the need to constantly update others on every pedestrian, mind-numbing detail of their lives? No, we don't care that you scarfed down a Burrito Bowl @ Chipotle today. We don't care that you got fifteen free moving boxes on Craigslist. We aren't interested in knowing that your six-year-old just earned his yellow belt in tae kwon do. And no, we are not fascinated by your musings on how Lady Gaga is the Dorothy Parker of our age.

The "Relationship status" feature is equally unhelpful. My favorite: "it's complicated." No, it isn't. You're either married or not, dating or available. And don't you love people who change their status multiple times a day? Their love lives can't be that interesting. Undoubtedly, their most meaningful relationship is with their computer keyboard.

Your Mother, Your "Friend"

The latest crisis facing university students is not what to major in, but what to do when Mom and Dad finally take the plunge into the world of social networking. Only when parents start following their college-age kids on Facebook do they really understand what a total waste that $50,000/year tuition payment truly is.

The seven most dreaded words that any freshman can read: "Mom wants to be friends on Facebook." He hurriedly goes to his "wall" to review his recent postings. In one photo, he's flipping the bird to the camera with his right hand, and is cradling a bottle of Smirnoff in the other. It might not have been so bad if he wasn't also standing atop a pyramid of half-dressed co-eds wearing football helmets. In another, he is lying on a ping-pong table with his lips wrapped around a beer funnel connected by a long clear tube to a pony keg. There's the one of him walking through the quad in his boxer shorts—barefoot, through the snow. The best is the invitation he posted to Tau Kappa Epsilon's annual "Strip & Flip Night," with an attached photo of him hanging off a stripper pole—half naked.

Now he faces the ultimate test. He could "accept" Mama into his online world, which would require that he scrub the R-rated photos he worked so hard to post. Or he could "Deny" her, which would set off her alarm bells and raise too many questions. When you go down the Debauchbook route, you're only really comfortable accepting peers and strangers into your online circle. At nineteen, showcasing photos of your *Animal House* escapades may seem like harmless fun, but when you're twenty-five and looking to impress a potential employer, they could come back to haunt you. For some, saving face may requiring keeping yours off Facebook altogether.

Losing the Farm

What would possess an otherwise normal person to give up precious hours and hard-earned money to assume the role of a virtual farmer? FarmVille, a ridiculous online farming game, has seduced fools around the world to cast aside family, obligations, and even their health in the pursuit of digital blue ribbons and co-ops. The kicker is they spend real greenbacks to expand their farming empire. FarmVille gamers blow $100 million annually to purchase tractors, seeds, and animals—that don't exist! They're digital! While their fake crops on FarmVille are thriving, their personal lawns are turning brown. These "farmers" will spend a fortune buying electronic dairy farms, but won't get off their duffs to buy their family a gallon of milk. For some, it has become an addiction and a distraction from life.

One husband lamented on a message board: "My wife spends endless hours on FarmVille and has forgotten about us, and the worst part is, she won't admit it. Our kids aren't fed, they go to school dirty ... wanna divorce? Start Farmin'!"

For those not inclined to go broke on digital Green Acres, there are other games available from Zynga, the company that created FarmVille. If you want to squander your cash on nonexistent buildings, why not waste your time in CityVille? This is another money pit posing as a game that casts you as a mayor who oversees the building of a sprawling city. For what it costs you to play, you could bankroll a genuine mayoral campaign in your own town! And for that stay-at-home-mom with a murderous streak: why not drop some cash assembling your own criminal syndicate in Mafia Wars? Though you may want to off yourself, once the bill comes. According to the *Sydney Morning Herald*, Zynga earned $850 million in revenue last year.

Want to make some real money? Come up with a twelve-step program to get people off these games. Only make it virtual, so the addicted will be sure to show up.

Match.Bomb

The stigma is finally gone from online dating. Everyone I know who is single is on one of the following: Match.com, eHarmony .com, Catholicmatch.com or Jdate.com. People who are sick of the bar scene, bad fix-ups, or just being alone have found that it's a fun and safe way to meet people. I know three terrific couples who met each other on Match.com.

So about ten years ago, at the urging of my producer, I decided to sign up myself. I will never forget my first "match."

"Robert's" online profile seemed interesting—a Russian major and swimmer in college, a voracious reader, and conservative who regularly attended church. He was the oldest of six and grew up in the South, which I thought would be a good balance for me (youngest child, New England upbringing). The photo he posted on Match.com was a little blurry (which I only later learned was a telltale sign of trouble). But from what I could make out he seemed to be attractive, with blondish wavy hair and brown eyes. For "height" he listed six feet one, for "build" he listed "athletic," and for "occupation" he listed "other profession." We had emailed back and forth for a few days and his witty repartee made it an easy "yes" when he asked me to meet him for lunch the following Saturday. Lunch was safe, not a big-time commitment and no date-like pressure.

When I arrived at the crowded downtown tapas joint, I scanned the room and I didn't see him. It was mostly twenty-somethings and young families—except, that is, for the man sitting in the booth near the window, staring at me. He started to get up and I thought—this can't be Robert. He looks nothing like the man I "met" online. "Robert" was tall and slim. This man was maybe five feet seven with a really bad reddish comb-over and small, round John Lennon–type glasses. Robert described himself as "athletic." This guy had a body type like Danny DeVito's.

I know what you're saying: "Laura, how sadly superficial! He could have been a great guy!" Call me crazy, but I don't think it's a good idea to start a friendship, let alone a relationship, with someone who misrepresented himself before he even met me. I wanted to turn on my heels and run, but instead I froze. He reached to shake my hand. "Hi, you must be Laura. I'm Robbie." His hand was drenched with perspiration, and I realized there was no escaping. The only adult "Robbie" I had ever heard of was the Band's great guitarist Robbie Robertson, who wrote one of my favorite songs, "The Weight." How appropriate.

Within ten minutes I learned that Robbie's hobby (he actually referred to himself in the third person) was studying famous Russian military campaigns, such as the Battle of Stalingrad. I felt like crawling out of my own skin when he described his "true passion" (!!)—painting and positioning small figurines representing the Russian and German armies. Oh, and given that he was "in between jobs," I realized this was also his "other profession." This was the longest seventy-five minutes of my life.

Apparently, the online fraud has gotten worse—a close thirty-two-year-old friend tells me of men she met on Match who lied about their ages (by twenty years!), their race (as if she wasn't going to find out!), and even their marital status. She noticed that the cute lawyer she had met online a few weeks earlier had a tan line on his ring finger. "My wife and I are on the way to being separated," he confessed.

Then there are "personal essays" loaded with bad grammar and feminized phrasings. "I love quiet walks in the woods and cudling [sic]." And don't you hate it when men use multiple exclamation marks!!!!!!!!!! (For example, "If you're [sic] idea of a perfect evening is cooking together and then curling up to watch an old movie, you could be my match!!!!!!!!!!!") I just hopped on a new dating site called PlentyofFish.com and froze: "After taking our *chemistry test* we match you with personalities that lead to long lasting stable relationships. We match you with daters that will meet your emotional needs." Couldn't do it. So I went back to Match.com. When I started to look at men in my age group, I saw that they were all interested in women ages 25–35. Most of the ones interested in my age range were on average fifteen to twenty years older than I. One seventy-five-year-old "winked" at my profile. All I could think of was Milk of Magnesia and Ben-Gay on the nightstand.

MyLife.com ... *"Who's searching for you?"*

Now not only are we searching online for people we know, want to know, or don't know at all, but we're also desperately trying to find out who's searching for us. Sites like MyLife.com provide this important service. Memo: Rest easy, no one is searching for you. It's as if some folks out there have cyber-stalker envy. I look forward to the next "advancement" in social networking, where we can search for the people who are searching for other people searching for them. Or maybe I'll launch a new site called TheirLife.com. It will search out all the people who utterly reject social networking and have a bona fide social life.

Internet Scams

Check out your inbox and inevitably there will be an email from a dead relative, a foreign head of state, or a friend you've never heard of stranded in Europe. These tiresome Internet scams are about one thing: getting your money.

I always get the urgent email from the exiled Nigerian prince who hopes to bring me a "prize of $3 million dollars." But to get the money out of the country, he needs me to send him two hundred dollars. The first time I saw the thing I thought, "Why doesn't he just deduct the two hundred bucks from my prize?" Then comes my favorite part: "Send me the best address for me to deliver your prize and your cell phone number." Okay, sure thing. Here's a key to my house and my Social Security number, as well.

The other day, I received another barely intelligible email from somebody named Ernie. I don't know anyone named Ernie, but I read it anyway. Ernie was facing a rough situation. He went to "England in the UK" (as opposed to England in Africa), and while there was mugged. He asked me to send along some cash to pay his hotel bill. Ernie promised to pay me back upon his return. All he needed was my name, bank account number, and address. If Ernie is still waiting for me to respond, he's going to be stuck in "England in the UK" for a long, long time. Or maybe the Nigerian monarch could help him out?

Online Flights of Chancy

Better to go to the airport to buy your ticket in person than to attempt to purchase one online. I recently went online and found an inexpensive flight. Immediately, I rushed to book it. After spending thirty minutes of comparison shopping, typing my address, card number, departure dates, return dates, and the birthdates of everyone in my party, a message popped up: "Sorry, that fare is no longer available." At that point I wanted to book a cruise instead, but I decided to go for the next "available" flight. After going through the whole rigmarole for another half hour, same outcome: "Sorry, that fare is no longer available."

In desperation, I called the airline Help Desk. When I shared my online booking nightmare, the woman kept repeating, "May I suggest you return to our website and try again to book your flight? Occasionally there is a minor glitch in the system, but I'm sure you will be quite happy . . ." She was obviously reading her responses from a card. At first, she sounded vaguely Southern. But when she repeated the "May I suggest you return to our website" routine, I picked up an Indian accent. She was probably seated in a call center in Mumbai at 2 a.m. her time. I opted to test my theory.

"Where are you now?" I asked.

"At the airline Help Desk. Now where are ya' calling from?" (Nice try with the "ya," by the way.)

"I know you're at the Help Desk, but where is the Help Desk located?"

She kept trying to change the topic and return to a discussion of my ticket. Finally, I threw out the big question. Whenever I doubt whether I am dealing with an American or a foreigner, I have a foolproof quiz: "Remember the *Brady Bunch* episode when Peter threw the party for himself?" She had no idea what I was talking about. I hung up.

Mad Dash to Distraction

From BMW's website: "The entire World Wide Web in your BMW. Book opera tickets online, order literature from Amazon, or catch the final moments of an eBay auction. A worldwide first among automobile manufacturers, BMW offers you genuine internet access on board across Germany . . ."

But don't worry. The driver's-side Internet screen works only while the car is stationary—for now. You knew it was only a matter of time. Now the Internet invasion of our automobile dashboard is fully under way. Ford, Audi, Mercedes, and pretty much every automobile manufacturer are touting add-on premium packages that allow drivers to "stay connected" via the Internet. This seems especially ironic, as more states are enacting "distracted driving" laws banning texting and cell phone use that is not "hands-free." Even without in-dash Internet service, State Farm Insurance reports that 20 percent of drivers are now "DWW" (Driving While "Webbing").

Then there are the "IWWs" (Idling While Webbing): most notorious are the drivers on smartphones who are oblivious when the red light in front of them turns green. I'm always behind them when I am in a desperate rush, or have to go to the bathroom. Honking has no effect, because these people have the music in their earbuds or car stereos turned up so high, they couldn't hear Christina Aguilera if she were singing to them from the passenger seat. Smartphones, dumbpeople.

Automobile and cell phone manufacturers hilariously contend

that the "voice command" features of their services will actually make driving less dangerous! Applying that logic, why not install a dashboard gin dispenser? They could market it as a safer option, because drivers will now be able to avoid the perils of rummaging around for their flasks.

Then there's the "my car is my office" justification for each new tech encroachment. Does this mean we should defend drivers' urinating in empty water bottles or relieving themselves in "mobile bedpans"?

"But officer, I wasn't distracted on the exit ramp! I was just using my 'office' restroom!"

The Announcers

I think some public cell phone users believe they are performing at Carnegie Hall. They project as though an invisible audience in the nosebleeds were having trouble hearing them. I was in line at a take-out café at Union Station in Washington recently where a young woman was speaking on her cell phone in front of me. She belted out: "I was, like, that's all you givin' me for my twenty-first birthday? And he was, like, 'Hello! I took you to Shoney's on Saturday.' And then I was, like, 'Duh! That didn't count. Fool!'"

Being forced to listen to her insipid and ungrammatical conversation was bad enough. The added insult was when I asked my friend what kind of soup he got and the cell phone screamer "shhhhh'd" me!

The volume of these cell phone barkers is often so high, they hardly need a phone to communicate at all. The person on the other line could just as easily hear them by opening a window. And it's even worse when the cell shriekers are speakerphone junkies: people who decide to place both sides of their conversation on public display. I am somehow always seated next to this type of person in a nail salon or on a train. If there's an enclosed public space and I'm in it, the speakerphone freak will find me. I once asked a fortyish woman if she wouldn't mind taking her phone off speaker since my (then) two-year-old son could overhear her entire conversation about menopausal hot flashes. Appalled at my request, she replied in the most serious tone, "Sorry, but I'm concerned about cell phones and cancer." A cancer cell wouldn't have a chance against that thick skull.

PDAs and PDIs

Bad cell phone and PDA behavior is so prevalent that it has its own acronym: Public Display of Insensitivity (PDI). A Web survey by a group called VitalSmarts found that 91 percent of those polled said they had suffered some cell phone–related PDI. (The other 9 percent must be hermits.) In addition to speaking loudly on cells, there are those people who brazenly check email during important meetings, and others who basically put their communications above the concerns and comfort of everyone else around them. Every day on the way to work, I witness multiple PDIs as I drive past dozens of individuals walking in crosswalks (with a solid red "Do Not Walk" sign illuminated), wearing earbuds, drinking or eating, and bellowing into their cell phones all at the same time. Oh, and if they have two cell phones, they are texting on the other one. These are modern-day Pod People. Honking at them is pointless, because they can't hear past their self-created digital cocoon. What we need is an engineer to develop a new add-on device for automobiles that will send out an electric jolt to PDAs in crosswalks. Think of it as an invisible fence for humans.

Porn Pilot

Cell phone cameras are fantastic gadgets. They allow us to capture those fleeting moments when a traditional camera would take forever to fish out. In a pinch, they're a wonderful way to quickly share images with family and friends. But getting a nude photo of someone you barely know standing in front of a mirror is not one of the images we had in mind.

"Sexting" is the transmission of explicit to downright pornographic images (usually self-portraits) via a cell phone or the Internet. The practice is so pervasive among teens that states like Texas and New Jersey are attempting to decriminalize sexting for youngsters. Should these efforts fail, the kids would have to be charged with possession of child pornography (since the images are usually of themselves or acquaintances), an offense that could get them added to the registry of sex offenders. A study by *CosmoGirl* and the National Campaign to Prevent Teen and Unplanned Pregnancies found that "20 percent of teens and 33 percent of young adults ages 20 to 26 have shared nude or semi-nude pictures of themselves either by text or posting online." According to studies, teen girls are more likely to indulge in the practice.

Sweetie, unless your ambition is to be the *Playboy* Playmate of the Month, might I suggest that you spend a bit more time adding to your résumé and a bit less time photographing yourself in the buff? This whole sexting thing has become a type of courting ritual. The fellows want to eye up the merchandise to see if you're worth the effort. As an old chef once said, "A sure way to kill the appetite is to give away too many hors d'oeuvres."

But the teens are only partly to blame for the explosion of sexting. They are merely mimicking what they see their heroes doing. In early 2011, nude pictures and videos of music star and woman beater Chris Brown surfaced online. Brown claims an ex-girlfriend leaked the material, though some reports suggested that he may have leaked them himself as a publicity stunt. NFL legend Brett Favre went for his own three-point conversion when he allegedly sent photos of his upright to a Jets "game day hostess." And more than fifty Hollywood A-listers were stunned when hackers stole their nude photos off cell phones and computers. Some of those hit included Jessica Alba, Miley Cyrus, Scarlett Johansson, and Christina Aguilera. All of this could have been avoided had they not taken the shots in the first place. By their example, stars have encouraged this cultural narcissism masquerading as courtship. It's not flirty, it's filthy—and it always leaks out.

There was a time when people got dressed up and had conversations to see if they were compatible—now they examine tan lines. Though there could be one advantage to the exposure: people will develop a new esteem for the option of seeing you clothed. I was recently told about one girl who tried to laugh off the nude picture of her circulating on campus. She announced to a college guy who had seen one of her salacious photos, "Bet you didn't know I was a natural brunette." To which the guy replied, "I didn't know you had stretch marks on your hips, either." If you're actually interested in the guy, clothing can be your closest ally.

When Nature Calls

You're on the phone with someone when unexpectedly, in the background, you can vaguely make out the sound of running water. Suddenly the whir of a hand dryer intrudes on your call.

"Where *are* you?" you ask.

"Just walking through the airport."

Yes, but which part of the airport? Don't let them deny it, you have just been taken to the bathroom. Cell phone etiquette commandment number one: don't take the cell phone anywhere you would not take the person on the other end of the line.

I wouldn't go into the men's room with you, and I don't want to go there virtually, either. We don't want to hear your voice reverberating off the bathroom stall, like Darth Vader. We don't want to hear your colon and bladder functions. And we certainly don't want to hear the sound of men grunting or flushing. Either get off the line or wait until you have finished your business before making a call. And no, I don't feel bad for the people who drop their cell phones in the toilet. You know they were GWP (Gabbing While Peeing) and they deserve to lose all their contacts and photos.

Think Before You Borrow

Consider the entry above before you press your cheek against your friend's BlackBerry.

Ring Drones

A few weeks ago, I decided to drop into church for a quick prayer before picking my daughter up from school. Some other mothers had the same idea. Just as I bowed my head the church's silence was shattered by Amy Winehouse, singing, "I told you I was trouble / You know that I'm no good." A few rows up a woman frantically rifled through her bag, trying to still the noise. She wasn't successful, and Winehouse again filled the church via the elusive cell phone. Women started looking for the exit. I wanted to tell the offender, "Go on, let it play. We don't mean to disturb you."

Few cell phone sins are as serious as the poorly chosen ringtone. First of all, there should be no ringtones. Phones should generically ring or vibrate, period. Now public spaces are filled with off-color movie lines, weird calypsos, and totally inappropriate sounds every time a cell phone rings. Marvin Gaye's "Sexual Healing" might have seemed funny when you bought your ringtone at the wireless store, but when you are pushing the kids in the shopping cart at the grocery and people have to hear, "Get up, get up, let's make love tonight . . ." it might be time to rethink your selection.

Several months ago, I was at lunch with a staffer on Capitol Hill. He seemed a great guy: smart, articulate, well dressed, and really knew his stuff. Then the cell phone went off: "I like big butts and I cannot lie . . ."

I looked up from my pasta, laid down my fork, and said one word: "Classy."

Whether it's jarring rap lyrics or nouveau romantic songs like Enrique Iglesias's "Tonight I'm F#%*ing You," don't subject us to your juvenile ringtone stupidity. If you want to listen to trash, be my guest—but wear headphones.

Cell phone etiquette commandment number two: the phone is not a PA system, and you are not a programming executive. Stick with a simple ringtone and leave the song and movie clips to the folks at Hulu.

Pocket Dialing

If you own a cell phone, you have either committed this act or have been victimized by it. Here's how it happens: You throw your purse down on the chair of a restaurant and your poor Aunt Anne gets a call that sounds as if you are speaking to her from the bottom of an elevator shaft. Aunt Anne can just barely make out the sound of your voice, given that the cell phone receiver is pressed up against stray Tic-Tacs and lint at the bottom of your purse. In desperation, Aunt Anne yells your name. But you can't hear her voice any more than the animals could hear Horton's Whos. A very agitated Aunt Anne hangs up the phone, which immediately calls her back—all night long.

Welcome to the world of pocket (or butt) dialing. This occurs when your cell phone's "Recently Called Number" function repeatedly dials whoever is at the top of your contact list. At other times it happens when you unwittingly have put contacts on speed dial. The moment you put the phone in your jacket, purse, or pocket, pressure is applied and the calls are made automatically. It isn't until weeks later, when Verizon sends you a bill for hundreds of dollars' worth of additional minutes, that you even know what happened.

I have a friend in Los Angeles who routinely calls me at 1 a.m., apparently whenever he goes to the clubs. Why can't he call from the opera or a poetry reading? At least I'd get some enjoyment out of it. By morning, my voice mailbox is full of messages containing pulsating music and muffled voices in a crowd. There is only one way to spare your friends and family from encountering these horrors: lock your phone down before you throw it in your purse or pocket. The other solution is to remove me from your contact list—which I hope Mr. Club Scene will do now, please.

The Power to Ignore

Of all the many problems I have with cell phones, there is one splendid feature that I happily use every day: the "ignore" function. There is nothing more empowering than seeing the name of a bothersome bore on the cell phone—requesting something for the sixth time that you've already said you won't do—and simply choosing to ignore him. Not only do you get the thrill of shutting down communication before it begins, but there is also the added satisfaction of making him sit through your chirpy voice mail greeting.

Endless Chargers

Over the last decade, I bet I have topped at least three landfills with just the cell phone chargers that I have lost, mislaid, or thrown out. Like maids who leave chocolate on the pillows, I leave a cell phone charger at every hotel I visit.

Rather than allow one universal charger to power all your devices, each phone manufacturer has designed its own unique port. I have a drawer at home where I keep all the charger cords. Opening it is like peering into the snake house at the zoo—you force yourself to look, but you wish you didn't have to. I usually approach the drawer whenever I return from a trip. I shove my hand into the tangled mess, hoping against hope that one of these cords will fit my phone. It never works. None of them ever fit. The only solution is to race down to the phone store and buy another charger.

"It's $29.99," the salesperson told me.

"Thirty bucks!? How much did I pay for the phone?"

After a few clicks on the computer in front of him, the guy smiles and says, "Well, first of all, the charger is not $30, it's $29.99. Second, your phone was free because you bought a two-year service plan."

"So let me get this straight: now the charger costs more than the phone I am using it to power." I did the only sensible thing: signed up for another two-year service plan, and got a backup phone and a free charger out of the deal.

Mistexting

A friend I've known for years would occasionally text me about something happening in her life or a news event. We weren't close, but we did stay in touch. She was a straight shooter and someone I had always gotten along with. Then one night, a string of accusatory text messages began to arrive from her, out of the blue.

"Are you ever going to call, a#$%*@e?" At first, I thought she was being funny, so I responded that I was sorry it had been so long since we last had contact. About ten minutes later I get this: "You're nothing but a f$#@ing @#&^! A liar and an a#@$*(e."

So I wrote: "Where is this coming from? Are you okay?"

The response: "I never want to speak to you again. And if I hear you say one thing about me I'll f!&k you over so bad you'll wish you were dead. A@(*&e!." That's when I picked up the phone and called her. I thought maybe she was off her meds or something. When the woman answered, she was sobbing. Turns out, my name appeared just before her boyfriend's in her contact list. She was in the act of breaking up with him at the time. In her emotional state, she texted me accidentally, thinking she was texting the soon-to-be-ex.

You thought SMS stood for Short Messaging Service? It should mean: Start Messaging Sober.

Auto Correcting

There is no more insidious feature on a cell phone than "auto-correct." Once engaged, it is supposed to catch our mistakes before they happen and repair all spelling errors. But as anyone who has tried to type a message without disabling auto-correct knows, the feature often causes more mistakes than it remedies.

For instance, a girl receives a text from a friend: "My dad was all over me tonight. I told him we had to wait. But when he kissed me, I kind of enjoyed it." You can imagine what the recipient thought of this. Auto-correct had merely changed "date" to "dad." Big difference. Thankfully, they caught it before the friend called Child Protective Services.

Auto-correct slipups happen all the time. Imagine the poor parents who received this text: "Harry is in the hospital. He took a terrible spill, but the doctors say he'll wake soon. I'll call you as soon as he dies." The text was meant to read: "I'll call you as soon as he *does*."

The *Oregonian* published this auto-correct nightmare:

> "Your Mom and I are going to divorce next month."
>
> *"What?? Why? Please call me!"*
>
> "I wrote DISNEY and this phone changed it.
> We are going to Disney (next month)!"

_____

The following gems come courtesy of Damnyouautocorrect.com:

"A little scared about this midget stiff but trying to stay positive and not let it get me down . . . BUDGET STUFF not midget stiff . . . damn Iphone self correcting stuff."

———

". . . Just went to the bookstore and got my colostomy bag!"

"I'm ready but what's with the colostomy bag?
And why is the bookstore selling them?"

"Seriously I typed COLLEGIATE FLAG.
I do not own a colostomy bag."

———

To avoid embarrassment and ridicule, follow the Ingraham rule of thumb on auto-correct. Before you send it, re-roof it. Ahhh . . . RE-READ it!!

Write as You Speak,
Write as You Text—OMG!

Phone calls are history. What telegrams were to my generation, the phone call has become to the current one. When the young want to communicate, they send a text—and it shows. How did a condolence message go from "I am so sorry to hear about John's passing. Know that we are all praying for you" to "Srry Jn died :(Prayin 4 U." Can't you just feel the sympathy?

According to the Nielsen Company, teens send an average of 3,339 text messages a year, or 107 a day. The text shorthand they use could not be more exasperating, particularly when adults try to appear cool by mimicking it. LOL (Laugh out loud), RTFL (Roll on the floor laughing), and OMG (Oh my God) have now given way to JEALZ (Jealous) and FOMO (Fear of missing out). As amusing as it is to try to figure out what the latest acronyms ultimately mean, there is a price to pay—and the young seem to be the ones paying it.

I have read numerous articles that suggest that texting actually helps enhance the communication skills of the young. Their teachers disagree. It turns out the kids' text habits and indecipherable lingo have started to turn up in schoolwork. According to the Associated Press, one teen's report on *Romeo and Juliet* read like this: "i luv Romeo & Juliet cuz u get to c how in luv the 2 caractrz r :p." Imagine the literary future that awaits this Hemingway. Washington State teachers told the AP that students are routinely "abbreviating and leaving vowels out of words." What did we expect? They are writing the way they habitually write to friends each day—like morons.

Guys, how about trying to be really countercultural? Why not give literacy a try? Not only will it make you look smarter, but others might actually be able to understand your ideas. By the way, "n" is never a substitute for "and." TAF (That's all, folks).

The Late-Shifters

Girls, when a man is texting, calling, or Facebooking you long after business hours, suggesting a last-minute, evening get-together, he's probably interested in one thing. Don't start humming "Here comes the bride." It's more like "Here comes the booty call." Smarten up, and don't reply. Not even Domino's delivers after 11 p.m.

Emoti-Nots

One of the biggest cop-outs of all time is the emoticon. :(These are the ridiculous smiling ☺ or frowning ☹ icons that writers insert into the body of their text messages. It is an implicit admission that you can't convey your emotions; spare us your attempts at graphic art. If I want to read a picture book, I'll go out and buy Dr. Seuss. Stop perverting punctuation marks and find a way to elicit honest emotion from the reader. You can start by writing a well-structured, moving sentence (>_>).

Remote Hell

One expects to find some escape from technology at home, at least in one's den. Don't look to my house. My children love to play a delightful game: hide the remotes from Mommy. There are four remotes for every TV in the house; one to operate the TV, another for the satellite system, still another for the receiver, and a skinny one for the DVD player. Misplace any one of them, and the TV could be out of service for days. Occasionally, I have to wander over to neighbors' houses just to watch a show I need to see for work.

Yet even if all the clickers are accounted for, it takes only one child punching buttons on a remote for the whole system to go haywire. Suddenly nothing is on the screen but snow. The DVD is working, but you can neither see nor hear it. After days of hitting every button on all four remotes, in desperation you call the satellite company.

A slack-jawed man always shows up at the door and asks the same thing. "Did you read the owner's manual?"

"You need a degree from MIT to read the owner's manual. I think I read the Quick Setup card inside the owner's manual."

"Well, you should have read the owner's manual."

"It's in four languages—none of them mine. I was lucky to make it through the Quick Setup card. Now, could you help me here?"

He presses a few buttons and within minutes everything is up and running. But within an hour, the dog has sat on a remote, and the thing is offline again. I spend the night reading the owner's manual, which says absolutely nothing about dogs sitting on buttons and disabling the system. The sickos who ran the wires to prisoners' genitals at Abu Ghraib could have saved themselves the trouble. If they really wanted to torture people, all they had to do was lock them in a room with a flat-screen, four remotes, and a dog.

7

Are We Having Fun Yet?

There was a time when I actually looked forward to recreating. No more. Now the stress of just planning an outing negates any possible enjoyment I could derive from it. But on those rare occasions when I do manage to make plans, to do something "fun"—it usually leaves me stressed-out and exhausted.

Relaxation is not for sissies. Whether you're seeking some downtime at a restaurant, the gym, a theme park, a movie theater, or even a museum, beware. Booby traps lie in wait, ready to frustrate your leisure at every turn. My blood pressure actually rises when I am attempting to recreate. I know I am not alone. But should having fun be this hard?

The 4 Habits of Very Bad Restaurants

For any discriminating restaurant patron, it is imperative to spot the signs of a grim culinary experience before it occurs. What follows are some telltale signs of eatery nightmares that I have collected through experience. Should you encounter any of the scenarios described below, head straight for the exit and don't look back.

* When you approach a nearly empty restaurant and the "hostess," on her cell phone arguing with her boyfriend, has the gall to ask, "Do you have a reservation?"—it is time to leave. I have a huge reservation—about walking into this hellhole in the first place. Glancing at the vacant tables I usually say, "Do I need a reservation? Are Bono and the band stopping by later?" That's when the hostess simulates checking her computer screen and says, "Here we go. We have a table for you. How many in the party?" The only thing to say at that point is, "None," and walk out.

* You should never enter a restaurant where the lighting is too bright. When your intimate dinner for two feels like an interrogation session at Guantanamo, it's time to vacate. Friends once took me to a swank restaurant in San Francisco. It had white tiled floors, mirrors on the walls, and lights everywhere. I think I got retinal damage before the appetizers came. Some places require men to wear jackets—these restaurants should require sun visors

and umbrellas. Restaurant lighting should be dim and soothing, not like a dentist's office during a root canal.

- When you first walk into an establishment, make sure you check the portion sizes on the tables. To save money, some restaurants are reducing portions to such a degree that each dish should be accompanied by a magnifying glass and a set of tweezers. I've seen steak medallions that should have been called steak pennies—they are so tiny they slide right through the fork prongs. Then there's the bowl trick: effete restaurants now serve wildly expensive cream of porcini mushroom bisque in a bathtub-sized bowl, with a mere film of soup coating the bottom. And let's not forget the garnish trick: restaurants that serve seared tuna the size of a thimble surrounded by a glaze sunburst and sprigs of grass. If you see serving dishes large enough to steal cable television signals and food portions too small for a gerbil, thank the hostess and find another restaurant.

- As odd as this sounds, always visit the bathroom before approaching the hostess stand at a restaurant. A friend of mine, from a venerable New Orleans restaurant family, once told me that his father used to clean the toilets of their establishment every day. "The kitchen is no cleaner than the bathrooms in a restaurant. So make sure both are always spotless in here," the founder of the restaurant advised his son. He's right. Next time you enter a restaurant, peek into the bathrooms and then take a trip to the kitchen. Filthy commode, filthy kitchen—it never fails. If the bathrooms have water everywhere, toilet paper strewn about, and filth on the fixtures, I don't care how renowned the restaurant is, I'm out of there.

Waiter Types

Generally speaking, there are two types of waiters: the ones who want to start an intimate relationship with you and the ones whose attention you couldn't get with flares and a siren.

- *The Smotherers:* These waiters approach the table like this: "I'm Julian and I'll be your server today—my, that is a fabulous color on you. It really brings out those baby blues . . ." You desperately want to say, "Julian, I came here for food, not for an escort. I don't care if your name is Julia Child, we'll get along fine if you just bring the bread."

- *MIAs:* These waiters greet you after you're seated, take your order, and then vanish. It's as if they passed into the Bermuda Triangle of the kitchen, never to be seen again. Even if you are lucky enough to catch a glimpse of them on the other side of the dining room, there is no use trying to get their attention. I have tried waving, whistling, using napkin finger puppets, even sending other waiters after them, to no avail. They seem to enjoy watching your desperate struggle for their attention. By the end of the attempted culinary encounter, you feel like a spurned lover. Explanations concerning their whereabouts are often hard to come by. My advice: find another waiter, order another meal and file a missing persons report before you leave.

- *The Hoverers:* These waiters whisk the food to the table while it is still piping hot. Then just as you take your first bite, the waiter starts to hover. "How's that foie gras? Isn't it delectable?" Of course, you can't speak because your mouth is full of unmasticated foie gras. You try to smile, wave, or give him a thumbs-up. But the waiter remains there with a quizzical look on his face. Short of spitting the food into a napkin, you manage a "Mmmmmmm. Verrrrrr. Gooooo." That is usually enough to appease him, buying you a few moments of peace. It won't last long. By the fifth bite, the waiter is sure to return.

  "May I take your plate away?" (Never mind that it's half full and others are still eating.)

"No, I'm actually still working . . ." By that time, you're trying to spear carrots in midair because the plate is floating away, en route to the kitchen. Though I have to say, I prefer the dish snatchers to those waiters who allow the empty plates to remain on the table until mold grows on them.

Tableside Soliloquies

Your friends kept telling you about the five-star restaurant that you "have to try." After repeated attempts, you finally score a reservation and settle into a table by the window. In the candlelight, it is all but impossible to read the menu. Then just as you start to squint and tilt the page toward a light source, it starts. There's no reason to read the menu, after all. Your waiter has arrived tableside to offer a dramatic interpretation of the entire bill of fare.

"What fish do you recommend?" you ask.

"You might favor the Wild Striped Bass—a house signature. Each fillet is hand wrapped by our chef in seaweed before steaming. Once it reaches the optimal temperature, the swaddled bass is drowned in a clear white wine sauce infused with clams, albino mushrooms, and organic baby potatoes. Before delivery to your table, our team tops the dish with a homemade sea salt butter finished with flecks of parsley garnish. I can tell you, it is a rare and explosive dish of pleasures."

I almost wanted to light up a cigarette.

If the entrée rundown is that verbose, you can bet the dish is going to be lousy. It's one thing to endure the over-the-top descriptions if the food is complex and original, but what happens when you ask the waiter if the burger is any good? Instead of a simple yes or no, you get a Rachael Ray episode:

"First you should know that all of our beef is one hundred percent certified Angus. Today the chef is featuring American Kobe, grilled to perfection, served on a seven-grain honey bun made on site each day. That comes with two slices of artisanal cheddar, diced red onion, Bibb lettuce, and a side of au jus to add moisture to your liking. Beer batter–encrusted onion rings are available for a small additional cost." English translation: the cheeseburgers and onion rings are good here.

Should you run across this variety of waiter/performance artist, don't ask for too many clarifications. By the time he's finished describing one item, your appetite will be gone, and you'll feel as though you have just sat through Shakespeare in the Park.

H_2 NO

It's always the waiter's first question: "Still, sparkling (then dropping his voice into a rueful tone) . . . or tap water?" To this annoying query I always answer: "Toilet, please." And why must they make such a production out of asking, "Do you want water?" What else are we going to drink while we wait for our food—ketchup? Of course we want water. Assuming it's tap, it's the only thing that's free.

If you happen to opt for a soda or iced tea in some restaurants, you may as well order wine. The moment the iced tea has been drained from the glass, the waiter will rush over to ask, "Can I get you another?" He isn't trying to be helpful. He's trying to run up the drink tab. Chances are, the same joints that sell the high-priced aqua don't do free refills. Bank on it.

The Customer Is Always Wrong

When a restaurant is new to me, I often ask the waiter a very simple question.

"What's good here?"

"Everything is good," he answers, immediately losing my trust by lying right off the bat. Take a stand. Surely you are more familiar with the fare served at your workplace than I. Sample the menu, give the customer some guidance, and bring the food out quickly. Otherwise when people ask, "Did you like that restaurant you visited last night?" I might well say, "Oh, all restaurants are good."

Patronizing Patrons

My mother was a waitress for thirty years, so I am always sensitive to the plight of servers. They don't have it easy. Dealing with the public is tough, and many times waiters and waitresses put up with hell for their tips. Not only is the job hard on the feet, it's also brutal on the nerves. Patrons can engage in absolutely hideous behavior, some of which I have observed myself.

- Some people just can't make up their minds. I always pity the poor waiter who literally has to wait while a customer studies the menu as if it were the Torah. It's not Aramaic, Mildred, just pick an entree and point. After seventeen minutes or so, they close the menu with great pomp and exclaim: "Gimme the roast chicken." For starters, "gimme" is not a word. Second, if you're going to order the chicken, skip the exaggerated menu inspection and save yourself the embarrassment.

- It's always sweet to see parents spending time with their kids, especially when they can share meals together. But when you bring the toddler to the restaurant, could you please order for him? There are few things more rude than a parent allowing the little one to order for himself—particularly when the child has yet to master speech. The waiter is not a gibberish decoder. "Go on tell the man what you want," one parent instructed his child, within earshot, as the waiter stood patiently by. "Go on, burrrrrr . . . burrrrr." This is not time for a phonics lesson. Just order for your kid and stop exhausting the waiter and your fellow patrons.

- If you're a vegan, don't go to a bar and grill. One night I was at a restaurant that specialized in steaks and burgers. A woman in the booth next to mine browbeat the waiter for a list of vegan dishes. When he tried to explain that there were salads and vegetables that she could order à la carte, the woman flew into a rage. "What century are you living in? I need a vegan entrée. We are not second-class citizens just because we don't eat animals." Well, at a steak restaurant, you are a second-class citizen if you don't eat animals. Just as a carnivore would be a second-class citizen at a tofu restaurant. Sorry that every establishment has yet to create a specialized menu for the vegans—but that's not the waiter's fault. I also love over-hearing people who request a detailed list of every ingre-dient in a meal and then add, "There are no peanuts or peanut oil used in the preparation of that dish, are there?" Not only is the waiter supposed to deliver your food, but now he also has to be a trained allergist.

- The kitchen staff and the servers had been on their feet for nearly twelve hours. The restaurant officially closed at 11 p.m. As I got up to leave with my party, at 10:50 or so, in streamed a group of last-minute patrons. You could feel the angst of the staff as they retied their aprons, fired up the ovens, and pulled everything out again for the latecomers. If you are going to go to an establishment near closing time, call ahead to see if they can accom-modate you. And as you fill your faces and guffaw until 1 a.m., glance over at the people on the other side of the room whom you are keeping from sleep and family. I know you're paying, but come earlier or come at another time. Restaurant workers have lives, too.

- And finally, if you can't afford to leave a tip of 18 to 20 percent of the bill, spend some time at home with the Gorton's fisherman. I know times are tough, but wait staff live on their tips. If they are working hard—and I remember seeing blisters on my mother's feet at the end of a long day—let them know they are appreciated. It's not only the decent thing to do, but it shows real class.

Food Courts

I know people have to eat, but must they congregate in food courts like livestock? I've never been a fan of the food courts. Sure they offer plenty of options, and it's an easy way to grab lunch on the run—but the victuals are universally bad and guaranteed to give you agita for several days. There are only four ingredients in anything served at a food court: sugar, salt, artificial coloring, and MSG.

And why is it that no matter what you order there, it all tastes the same? I'm convinced that a single company owns every storefront in the food court; six restaurants, one kitchen. All the food comes out of the same pot. The burgers at Five Sisters taste exactly like the General Tso's Chicken at the Wok & Rock—lousy!

Not even the father of our country has been spared the food courting of America. How proud George Washington would be to know that he repelled the British and established a new republic so a food court could be erected on his homestead. Washington's home, Mount Vernon, now has its own food gallery. The famous Mount Vernon peanut and chestnut soup has been overshadowed by personal pan pizzas and hot dogs. It's nothing short of a national tragedy. It would be like serving Dippin' Dots on Abe's feet at the Lincoln Memorial.

If I were judge of the food court, I would convict all these establishments on multiple counts of culinary fraud—with no parole.

Feeding Time

I recently took my children to the zoo. It was thirteen dollars a head just to get past the turnstiles—not counting the snacks, stroller rental, and the Excedrin packets I picked up on the way in. After gawking at the tranquilized elephants and gorillas, the hyenas and the zebras, we reached the farm exhibit. This is where livestock are allowed to wander in a gated yard, and the kids are encouraged to chase them with foodstuffs.

For thirteen dollars a head, you'd think they'd give you the animal food—I mean they have to purchase it anyway. No doing. The farm food costs a buck-fifty a cup. After three hours at the zoo, the animals should pay me for my efforts to stand upright.

It was obvious that the creatures had learned to hate human beings toting cups full of brown pellets. The sheep were sprinting away from every toddler in view. The goats looked downright furious. One was ramming a defenseless tot in the far corner of the yard. Hard as I tried to direct my children away from the attraction ("C'mon we're missing the porpoise show . . ."), they would not be dissuaded. I even tried bribing them with Happy Meals. Nothing worked. Finally, I decided to let the kids chase the animals for a bit and situated myself on a little stool in the shaded corner of the yard. As I sat there, two strange children ambled over and extended their feed cups in my direction. "I hope you don't think I'm paying you by the pellet," I told them.

The Death of Silence

Silence has become the enemy of our culture. No matter where you go, noise goes with you. An abusive soundtrack runs under every aspect of lives now. At times, it feels like we are extras in a Rihanna video, without the rehearsal or the paycheck.

Enter a hotel lobby—loud, thumping music overhead. Vivaldi I could abide. But when techno trash like Pitbull's "Hey Baby (Drop It to the Floor)" is filling a public space, it's enough to send you screaming into the streets. Then you imagine you might find some quiet in your hotel room. No sooner do you open the door than you are assaulted by the sound system on the nightstand, running at full tilt. And you can never figure out how to turn the thing off. In desperation, you jump in a taxi to find some solitude. A television embedded in the back of the driver's seat loudly replays excerpts of NBC's crummy lineup. You'd turn the thing off if it didn't require pressing the filthy screen.

Slip into a restaurant for a quiet meal, forget it. Loud music drowns out all conversation. Tables are filled with people shouting to be heard over the soundtrack. Those with hearing devices just turn them off and stare at the bread in frustration.

Go shopping, blaring soundtrack. Get into an elevator, blaring soundtrack. Go to the gym, blaring television. You can't even pump your gas in peace (as if paying $5 a gallon isn't torture enough). The moment you slide the credit card at the pump, a TV monitor on the thing begins assaulting you with highlights from CBS shows. Julie Chen and Letterman clips are not what I want to see while pumping gas. It's enough to make you pour gas on yourself and reach for a match.

The only place to find any solace is outdoors, or so you'd think. Recently I went for a walk in an outdoor mall in beautiful Fort Myers, Florida. What wasn't beautiful was the unwelcome reggae music on every block. Stores and restaurants not only fill their interiors with bad music, but have also taken to installing speakers on the street. So we can now seamlessly pass from one clamorous place into another.

On a recent trip, I decided to find some peace by taking a walk on the resort's outdoor nature path. Big mistake. No sooner did I step onto the path than I was jarred by music. What I wanted was quiet and tranquility, what I got was Bryan Adams and Michael Bolton in Surround Sound. It was like they were walking behind me. Outdoor speakers hanging from the trees and hidden in faux rocks blasted the raspy falsettos. The quivering woodland creatures appeared to be in need of psychological help. Can't Chip 'n Dale collect their nuts without accompaniment?

Gargantuan Green Lanes

Since 2006, New York City has added more than 250 miles of bike lanes. This is a town where it takes forty minutes to drive six blocks, if you don't get caught in rush hour—and city planners are worried about bike lanes?! Sadly, the answer is yes.

Mayor Michael Bloomberg envisions New York as a quaint European village; a place hostile to motorized vehicles, where only pedalers and bipeds need enter. Bloomberg has even transformed the "center of the universe," Times Square, into a pedestrian plaza and biking Mecca—shutting down all vehicular traffic on Broadway. They call this sooty set-aside a "green space." The only green things I ever saw there were discarded Starbucks cups and a few globs of bubble gum stuck to the street. Commuters idling for hours in the congested side streets surrounding Times Square are livid. But the mayor, who must helicopter his way around town, had this to say in a statement: "We created pedestrian plazas right in the heart of our City to straighten out some of the chokepoints in our street grid and to help traffic flow more smoothly and quickly through Midtown." I don't know what city he's talking about, but it sure is not New York. All of Midtown is now one big parking lot, east to west. But so long as Mayor Bloomberg is happy, there we are. His statement continued: "We also expected that by reducing the numbers of vehicles in and around Times Square, we would also improve the area's air quality, and that's exactly what the numbers now show." If the air in Times Square was so bad owing to the traffic, how does rerouting that same traffic to nearby neighborhoods improve the air quality? Wouldn't the new travel flow just make the air worse for those living on the streets around Times Square? Bloomberg didn't stop air pollution; he just relocated it.

Now the nation's capital is under attack by the pedal-pushing psychos. Pennsylvania Avenue, our national main street—the grand boulevard that the president traverses on inauguration days and for his State of the Union address—is now also choked by biking lanes. It would be one thing if they were discreetly off to the side, but the bike paths are smack dab in the middle of the street. They consume two lanes previously used by vehicles. I'm waiting for the Segway, Rascal, and Radio Flyer lanes that are no doubt in the planning stages.

The endgame of these city planners is clear: to eradicate motor vehicles—to make it so difficult to drive into town that we will turn to public transit, bike, walk, or just crawl to work. There is a glaring problem with their scheme. Almost no one is using these bike lanes. A study by NYU's Furman Center revealed that for all the dislocation and traffic, a pathetic .06 percent of New Yorkers actually bike to work—a 14 percent drop from 2007, when they didn't have nearly as many bike paths. In Washington, D.C., only 2.3 percent of people pedal to work. But don't write off the bike lanes yet. They do have a function. When the traffic really snarls, you now have a clear path to walk home on once you abandon your vehicle.

Segway to Disaster

I was exiting the ladies' room at the airport not long ago and was practically run over by a cop on a Segway scooter. He muttered a "sorry" as he blurred by, but he couldn't really look back, for fear of crashing into a Cinnabon stand.

These ridiculous, self-balancing, two-wheel contraptions have been sold almost exclusively to novelty collectors and law enforcement because, quite frankly, they have no other societal utility. There are people who marvel at the Segway's ability to balance itself on two wheels. Congratulations. For thousands of dollars, it has managed to duplicate the effect of training wheels on a bicycle.

In my opinion, there are a couple of reasons police officers should avoid riding these things. First, the Segway makes all riders look like comic extras in a Star Trek movie. Officers can convey no sense of authority on a Segway—they may as well be riding unicycles. Second, how much crime busting can a cop do at a maximum speed of 12.5 miles an hour? A kid on a Big Wheel could outrun you.

I don't even think these scooters are safe. In 2010, James Heselden, the owner of the company that produces the scooter, drove off a cliff in England while testing an all-terrain Segway model. Now if the owner, who presumably was familiar with the handling of the vehicle, died, should Aunt Suzy be gliding in and out of traffic on one in a strange city?

Go to any major city and you are likely to see rolling rows of helmeted tourists, like overfed ducks, taking in the sights.

A Segway excursion is for those who want to avoid the physical activity implied by the term "walking tour." Imagine the calories they'd burn if they stepped off the thing. And how pleasant it would be to stroll down a path without fear of a sidewalk hit and run.

Concession Obsession

Not only do you pay through the nose for the tickets and the parking at sporting events, but now you have to take out a third mortgage if you want to eat once you get there. We've gone way beyond peanuts and Cracker Jacks. I almost fell out of my seat when, during spring training at Salt River Stadium in Phoenix, a vendor came down the aisle hawking five-dollar chocolate-covered strawberries and bananas on a stick. They also had fancy barbecue, wraps, Mexican food, ten-dollar beer, and specialty desserts galore. "Is Emeril going to show up to cook something seat side for the regular-season games?" I wondered.

The luxury concessions trend is not confined to Phoenix. At Tampa's Tropicana Field, they now have wine tastings before Rays games. And once you pick the right chardonnay, you can head over to the Fresco Fish Tacos for delectables created, according to the *Tampa Tribune,* by Dave Pasternack, the seafood chef at Esca in Manhattan. Today, it's hard to know if you are at a professional sporting event or at a food expo. And you can always rely on the New Yorkers to kick it up a notch.

Yankee Stadium has a new "fresh to order" food policy. So now there is a Lobel's of New York preparing dry-aged steaks, in stadium. They sell New York strips to the box seats and steak sandwiches to the plebeians. Some people won't be happy until Mario Batali himself is taking orders and passing the pasta through the concessions pickup window. Only in the United States could a sporting event turn into a season of *Iron Chef America.*

Exorcising the Exercise "Crazes"

Raise your hand if you are tired of reading articles about the year's new "exercise trends"—as if we have to be endlessly entertained by our exercise and fitness regimens.

We've come a long way from Jamie Lee Curtis's "And five-six-seven-eight! And lift, and step, and lift and step!" I still remember my first aerobics class twenty years ago. I bumped into the perfectly outfitted and coordinated woman next to me, tripped over her "step," and was told not to come back until I took a "beginner's class." Humiliating for a former three-sport varsity athlete—the operative word being "former." Today things are even more daunting. Now we feel inadequate if we haven't experimented with "kettlebells" (are plain dumbbells now just for dummies?), Zumba (a Latin-style dance routine), Power Plate Pilates (involves a vibrating platform), or Yoga Booty Ballet (two out of three ain't bad).

Confused? Obviously, you haven't hired a personal "wellness coach" yet. He or she is meant to help you navigate the ever-complex world of physical fitness, and assist you in making the required "behavioral changes." (The first change? Get used to paying big bucks for someone to tell you stuff that I can tell you for free: eat less and exercise more.)

Besides celebrities such as Jennifer Lopez who are paid to look good in dresses that are two sizes too small, who exactly has the time to devote to this? Ladies in between carpool pickups? Men who want to pick up women who are in between carpool pickups? The "ladies who lunch" are now the "ladies at Crunch." An intimidating bunch.

A few years ago, I was curious about Pilates, so I thought I'd give it a whirl. So many of my friends swore by this low-impact, but challenging, stress-reducing workout. So I showed up at my health club one Saturday morning, and told the twenty-something at the front desk that I wanted to try the 10 a.m. class. With the most condescending look, she sniffed, "That class fills up by eight-thirty." Incredulous, I asked, "So I have to be here ninety minutes before it starts?" "No, eighty-thirty the night before," she laughed. Stressed out, I went home, did some push-ups and sit-ups, and ate a grilled cheese.

Men Who Take Trendy Exercise Classes

Don't. Women in the classes won't respect you; men who see you in the classes will ridicule you. Hit the bench press, dudes.

Unsolicited Advice

"You should watch your extension on that lift," a voice sounded behind me as I lay on the weight bench. I placed the dumbbells down and glanced back to find a pudgy middle-aged man in a compression shirt hovering over me. "If you take the weights up halfway, it'll protect your rotator cuff." I thought, "Who's going to protect your rotator when I cuff you?"

If I wanted a private trainer, I would have paid sixty dollars for one. But some men consider it their duty to offer unsolicited advice to any decent-looking woman in the free weights area. More often than not, the man claims to be a "former personal trainer." Judging by the looks of him, the "former" part is easily understood. The "trainer" bit is harder to process. But I suppose there are whale trainers, so maybe he is telling the truth. No matter what he may claim to be, I know what he is: just another horndog on the make.

Gym Clothes

I hate to break it to you, ladies, but a jog-bra isn't a shirt. The only thing worse than a woman on the next elliptical machine wearing a jog bra for a top is a man bouncing up and down in a gauzy singlet who should be wearing a jog bra. Do these guys think women find visible chest, underarm, and back hair attractive? Or did they just forget their T-shirt and are wearing the same b.o.-stained undershirt they wore all day at work? Next time, protect against visual blight and skip the workout altogether.

G.J.S. ("George Jetson Syndrome")

Then there are the gym rats who can't bear to be on the treadmill without their cell phones. You thought texting while driving was dangerous? A few months back, a thirty-something with a perfectly sculpted body was putting us all to shame on the treadmill. I had mine cranked up to a meager 6.8, and without breaking a sweat, he had to be running at an 8.0 clip. To top it all off, he was doing all this while tapping away at his BlackBerry. I went back to watching some hideous C-SPAN hearing on the room's big flat-screen television, when suddenly I heard a huge crash. Mr. Winged Foot was on the floor, and had been catapulted off the machine into the wall behind him. I kept thinking of George Jetson caught in his space treadmill, screaming: "Jane, stop this crazy thing!" Embarrassed, he tried to hop up quickly but had obviously hurt his foot. A tubby young gal helped him up.

"That phone's really dangerous! It flew onto my treadmill," she huffed, handing him his cell phone. "I almost tripped and flew off, too!"

"Oh, thank God . . . that my BlackBerry's all right," he said, furiously scrolling from function to function. That day he exercised everything but good manners.

Fair and Balanced Channel Surfing

Mystery solved! I have finally figured out how CNN and MSNBC (the #3 and #2 cable news networks, respectively) manage to draw any viewers at all, let alone hundreds of thousands at one time. Those numbers are artificially inflated by the captive audiences forced to watch their "snooze" casts in airports and health clubs!

Now I'm fighting back. Regardless of what gym I'm using, in whatever city I'm visiting, I take undue delight in making sure that at least one of the communal TVs is tuned to Fox News. If the health clubs are in Washington, Los Angeles, Manhattan, or D.C., this usually means picking a fight with some nasty progressive. I knew I was in for a scene a few weeks back when I spotted a pale, slight Gen-Xer, wearing a "Yes we can!" T-shirt, reading the *New Yorker,* and pedaling a stationary bike. He and his scraggly brown goatee seemed to be oblivious to all else around him—until, that is, I took the remote and switched the channel from CNN to Fox. Immediately, he blurted out, "Hey, I was watching that!" Without missing a beat, I shrugged my shoulders and quipped, "Just consider it 'change you can believe in.'"

I call this a "fair and balanced" approach to televisions in public places. The mere sight of Bill O'Reilly or Sarah Palin can make a lefty seethe. But they should thank me when I do the switcheroo. It's the only time I see any of them work up a sweat.

Sweat Hogs

Some people should come to the gym with their own splat mat. A few weeks ago, I was waiting to get on a treadmill, when the man using it finally stepped off. I patiently stood aside, anticipating that he would wipe down the equipment. Drops of his perspiration had created a film on every surface of the machine. After waiting several moments, I realized he was not coming back. Sop up your sweat when you are finished with a piece of equipment. It is unsanitary, and contrary to what you might think, your sweat does not smell like Coco Chanel!

After cleaning up Perspiring Peter's mess, I hopped onto the treadmill next to the weight area. Though I tried to read, it was impossible given the painful grunts and groans coming from the man on the bench next to me. This is not the power lift at the Olympics, okay? Unless you are giving birth or tending a grievous wound there is no reason to make sounds like that. Lower the weight and be quiet. At times, these guys lift a dumbbell and it sounds as if they're having a bowel movement. Then again, given the smell in there, maybe they are having a bowel movement.

You Are Not a Member of the Cast

The movie theater lobby was jammed with wizards and witches. As I walked in, I thought for a moment that a private costume party was under way. Though I had a ticket to an entirely different film, I had unwittingly wandered into the opening night of a new Harry Potter movie. Why do some people feel it necessary to dress as the characters in the movie to enjoy it? I mean, when people go to the opera on opening night, they don't come dressed as Carmen and Don José. And have you ever seen anyone at the U.S. Open costumed as, say, Venus Williams? But moviegoers are all about the masquerade.

Whether it's Star Wars, Harry Potter, or Hannah Montana, the die-hards are sure to be in costume. Standing next to the Potterites, I found myself wondering, "How is that guy breathing in his Voldemort mask? And will the woman in the witch hat be taking that thing off, or will they just seat her at the back of the theater?" Rows and rows of these people were dressed as various characters from the film. The only confusing "character" was a young woman near the end of the line who wore a blond bob wig and cream-colored sundress, and clutched a Harry Potter book. "Who are you supposed to be?" I asked. After expelling all the air in her lungs, she rolled her eyes and said, "J. K. Rowling. Duh!"

Unless you've been contacted by the film's casting director, there is no reason for you ever to come to a movie in costume. We don't think you're cute. We don't think you're artistic. We do think you're a nerd. And the moment you leave the protective company of the other crazy people at the cineplex, you look like a complete idiot. The robe and the wand are not working for you.

Oh, and the last time I checked, Harry Potter was not three hundred pounds, forty, or balding.

Coming Detractions

You've just spent fourteen bucks on a movie you'll forget in about ten minutes, but you figure it's an escape; a chance to get away— if not from life, at least from the humdrum offerings on television. You arrive at the theater on time, settle into your seat with your popcorn, and wait for the previews. You're looking forward to the coming attractions; exciting, fun films that will be opening in the next few months. Instead you get a commercial for MSNBC. No matter how far forward they lean, Chris Matthews and Rachel Maddow are not exactly enticing attractions. But the good news for my old network chums is, at least now they can claim to have an audience.

Movie previews have now been reimagined as just another commercial break. Sitting in the dark, you are punished by car commercials, Coke and Pepsi ads, and those ridiculous "Taste the Rainbow" Skittles ads. Then, just as it seems to be coming to an end and we're seeing actors again—it's a promotion for new TV shows. If I wanted to see commercials, I would have watched a movie on network television. At least at home I have the option of leaving the room, there is no extra charge for refills, and there's always toilet paper in the bathroom.

Reel Rude

Movies tend to bring out the worst in people. I don't mean their reaction to what they see on the screen—I mean the behavior they evince once seated in the theater.

One time I was watching a war epic intended for adults. It was rated R for its realistic depiction of violence. Some of the brutal visuals were very difficult to watch—like an episode of *The Joy Behar Show*. Two rows in front of me sat a husband and wife with their two children—the kids were no more than five years old. Since when has it become acceptable to take your children to adult movies because you're too lazy to hire a babysitter? This is why God made Redbox. Send your children to bed and watch the movie in the den.

I have also been to children's films where there are more adults than children in attendance. This seems a nice thing, until you realize that many of the couples are childless—yet there they sit in the middle of the afternoon, watching the antics of Yogi Bear and Boo-Boo. One questions the mental competency of such people. As a rational explanation for their presence, you almost hope they're on a bender. Many times, these are the same goofs who talk to the screen: "Ohh, look out behind you, Ranger Smith. Watch it. Watch it." Hey, Chuck Jones, the cartoon characters can't hear you—but we can. If real-time audio commentary is what we crave, we'll wait for the DVD, thank you very much.

Then there are the BlackBerry flashers. These are the people so uninterested in the movie that they start checking their BlackBerrys in the dark. If you happen to be looking in their direction when they fire the thing up, you could damage an iris. If the movie is a real snooze, half the theater begins checking BlackBerrys and iPhones. Suddenly the cinema looks like a landing strip at midnight.

The savagely rude will then make a phone call from their seat and begin a full-on conversation during the movie. I didn't pay fourteen bucks to hear your absorbing conversation about a sick cat. I came to see Colin Firth. Unless you're on the phone with him and he has a private message for me—turn the phone off and shut up.

The Permanent Collection

I've always thought it a good idea to expose children to fine art at a young age. On one occasion, I took my daughter to an art museum and walked her through some of the more colorful galleries. Like any five-year-old, she had an immediate reaction to what she was seeing. She laughed, asked questions, and even mimicked the sounds of the animals she saw in a few of the paintings. Suddenly, from the far corner of the gallery, an old woman, who looked as if she were part of the permanent collection, emitted a nasty "Sssssshhhhhhhh." What is this, a church service? Since when did the museum become a monastery—a place where children can't speak or allow art to affect them? This is the same old dame who chats up her bridge partner during the movie.

All over the same museum, there were people with their cell phones extended, recording every image in the gallery, muttering to themselves, and no one said a word to them. Americans now experience live events, art, and even family life via their cell phones. They're so busy watching life go by in the display screen that genuine human emotion and interaction are no longer a part of the equation. But a child squeals with delight at a piece of art, and it's a federal offense.

We have become experts at capturing images, but often fail to see deeply. Our children should be encouraged to have honest reactions to the world around them and not bullied into silence when they attempt to interact.

Decades from now, children of the future may no longer wish to visit museums. Their permanent collection could well be old cell phone snapshots, captured by today's adults, posted on some untended blog. As sad as that would be for our culture, at least the old biddies in the galleries won't have to worry about quieting the kids anymore.

The Free Museums

There is no tourist refrain in Washington that I enjoy more than "We're going to see the Smithsonians. I can't believe they're free."

Sure they are. So free, we all get to pay our admissions each April 15, whether we visit the Smithsonians or not. The nineteen museums, ten of which fill the National Mall, cost $761 million a year to operate. Sixty-five percent of that money comes from you, the American taxpayer. I can assure you, nothing in Washington is free. I think it's wonderful that we attempt to preserve some of our great art and chronicle America's gifts to the world. But aside from the Air and Space Museum, the National Portrait Gallery, the American History Museum, the Natural History Museum, and the American Art Museum, most Americans could do without the others—particularly the string of affirmative-action museums that are only spawning more unvisited, federally funded sites.

A presidential commission recently called on Congress to authorize the building of a National Museum of the American Latino. The cost? A pequeño $600 million. That's a lot of dinero for a Tex-Mex food court and a Gloria Estefan exhibit. And did you know that there is an American Indian Museum on the Mall, not to be confused with the other Smithsonian-run American Indian Museum's Heye Center in New York City? Plans are under way for the construction of a National Museum of African American History and Culture, despite the fact that the Smithsonian already has an Anacostia Community Museum in Washington that exists to preserve "African American history and culture." And incidentally, there is already an African Art Museum on the Mall. I can already hear the cries for an Irish American Museum, an Italian American Museum, and a Muslim American Museum/Mosque/Community Center. If these groups want to build museums to honor themselves, have at it. But raise your own funds, and don't saddle the taxpayer with niche projects that only a small group of tourists would ever want to visit. Though we could probably save ourselves a lot of money if we just build one huge Museum of Hyphenated Americans in the middle of the Mall. Or how about this novel idea: consider yourselves part of American history and lobby for space in the American History Museum.

It's a Gridlocked World, After All

After years of resisting, and asserting that I would "never do it," I finally gave in and went on my first trip to Disney World. Friends and I decided to make the trip between Christmas and New Year's. So many people made the same decision that three out of the four Disney parks—having reach maximum capacity—were closed at various times during our visit. What happened to the recession? It was Mickey mayhem from start to finish. Disney "cast members" and friends who have been going to the parks for thirty years said they had never seen crowds this dense. Leave it to me to visit the Magic Kingdom during two Florida bowl games, in the middle of the Christmas holidays. The "Happiest Place on Earth" was anything but.

Getting to the parks was like boarding a commuter bus to San Salvador. In the morning you joined a large queue outside the hotel in hopes of getting on the next shuttle. Then once the thing pulled up, you had to wait as a separate line for the disabled, and frauds posing as the disabled, boarded the bus. This operation took several minutes while ramps were extended and the parade of mobility scooters and wheelchairs was guided on board. Now, we should give preference to people who are truly disabled, but when you have just rented a Rascal because you are too lazy to walk, why should you get a fast pass? When we were finally allowed on board, children and adults had to turn into Cirque du Soleil performers to get around the strollers and the morbidly obese people already jamming the aisle. Next time I'll just ask to be strapped to the roof with some bungee cords. Though we were staying on the Disney property, it took us forty-five minutes to drive from the hotel to the parks. At two stops along the way, we were instructed to press together and move to the back of the bus to allow more visitors on. I thought, if we allow one more person on this bus I'm going to have to dangle my leg, my purse, and at least one child out the window.

The average wait time per attraction was an hour and a half. With the small children in our group, we were fortunate to enjoy five rides a day—assuming we cut our lunches short, which wasn't hard, since we couldn't get a reservation anyhow. And trust me, you don't want to be in the presence of a three-year-old who catches a glimpse of Snow White's gown through the restaurant window, only to be told by a "cast member," "I'm sorry, there is no available seating until next Thursday. Have a magical day."

The most distressing part of the adventure was trying to get from attraction to attraction. I have a real phobia of crowds. And even on wide thoroughfares like Main Street, the crowds were so dense, you could hardly move. Factor in the mobility vehicles stacked up in all directions, and it could have been a scene from *The War of the Worlds*.

People don't walk in Disney World anymore, they ride—and I don't mean on the Monorail. At least one member of every party is on some sort of mobility vehicle. When crowds are as thick as Rice Distribution Day in Calcutta, adding thousands of people with limited driving skills and plenty of tonnage is not a good idea.

Near the end of our trip, during the Electrical Parade, my daughter was pushed by the crowds and fell, hurting her lip. We got separated in the crowd, but thankfully she was with family friends across the street from me. When I tried to get to her,

I found myself blocked in by Rascal gridlock. All around me were people ramming their scooters into ankles and complaining about the traffic, even though they were its primary cause. After climbing over several scooters and ducking under some ropes, I finally made it to Maria, who, thankfully, was fine.

If I ever return to Disney, it'll be during off-season, and I'll be driving a Rascal with a battering ram.

8

Why Do the Wrong People Travel?

Americans love to travel, and I share the adventuresome spirit. I have been privileged to visit nearly every state in the union. I've traveled by car, rail, plane, and boat. With this vast travel experience, I can conclude: unless a relative has died or you are getting paid lots of money, there is no good reason to leave the house.

Each year travel becomes more burdensome and miserable. From the ever-changing TSA carry-on rules, to the gridlocked roads, to the lousy food on Amtrak, to the pungent passengers, the travel experience will mar your spirit (and your vacation). So put your seatback in an upright position, buckle up, and let's get going. We will be experiencing turbulence throughout this flight, so we regrettably cannot provide the usual beverage service.

(Translation: we're too lazy to push the drink cart down the aisle. If there's a real emergency, you can find us sitting on the jump-seats in the back of the plane, reading *People* magazine.)

Scuttle the Shuttle

The ordeal often begins long before you ever reach the airport or train station. It always seems like a good idea in theory: leave the car at home, save money on parking, and simply call up the airport shuttle service. I don't care if that van is blue, red, white, green, or fuchsia: don't get in. It is supposed to be a shuttle to the airport, but it ends up being more like an unplanned Gray Line tour from hell.

In Washington, you phone the shuttle service and you give them your airline and flight number. This is how the conversation goes:

DISPATCHER: "What time is your departure?"

PASSENGER: "Ten o'clock in the morning."

DISPATCHER: "Then we'll pick you up at 5:00 a.m."

PASSENGER (stunned):   "What? Why so early?"

DISPATCHER: "That's just our policy, ma'am."

I got the real answer after ninety minutes in the van. The airport shuttle needs the extra time for a scenic sunrise tour of your town and adjacent boroughs as it picks up all the other people who are flying in the same twenty-four-hour period. No matter what time, day or night, your plane is scheduled to depart, the pickup time's the same: 5:00 a.m. Not surprisingly, your fellow passengers are usually in foul moods. Half of them look like they belong on the TSA "Do Not Fly" list. I think they just ride the shuttle to and from the airport to reminisce.

With each shuttle stop, the horror intensifies. First comes the man who decided to skip the shower, but did opt to douse himself in Old Spice. Then a scruffster guy wearing a backward ball cap and a "Naked Lacrosse" T-shirt climbs aboard, scratching his nether regions. Next comes the senior citizen standing on her porch with a walker, eight trunks, and some sort of mobile iron lung. Getting this poor woman and her retinue on board takes at least twenty-five minutes. You could have walked to the airport faster. But then you would miss the charming driver who chats you up along the entire route: "So, that's a mighty nice house you live in? Real pretty. I noticed you didn't have a ring on your finger. Must get awfully lonely in a house like that for a pretty lady like you." Sandwiched between Old Spice and Mr. Doofus at 6 a.m., the "pretty lady" is seconds away from grabbing Granny's walker from the backseat and throttling the driver with it. All the while, one thought keeps running through my head: "In only four short hours, I'll be away from these people—confined to a metal tube in the sky with a whole new group of insufferable strangers." That's when we pull up to a shabby motel on the edge of town, where four people who appear to be members of MS-13 prepare to join our happy band. As they push their way onto our shuttle, the driver turns to me and says, "This is the best job in the world. You meet great people, have nice conversations, and the ladies are always pretty."

The Touchy-Feely TSA

If I need a massage, I'll schedule one. Being groped in front of hundreds of weary travelers by a TSA employee at seven in the morning is not my idea of a good time. It doesn't make me feel any safer, in fact it makes me feel less secure. I've heard the ads for a certain airline claiming "You're free to roam." These TSA people have taken it literally! This is their moment to get back at all those people who scored higher than they did on the SATs (or who took them at all). I know the Obama folks did away with the color-coded terror alert system, but maybe they should reconsider.

First, you have to shed your shoes and walk where thousands

of athlete's foot sufferers have trod before. (Be honest: have you ever seen anyone actually clean the floor alongside the conveyor belt or through the metal detector?) Then, should you make it down Fungus Alley to the filthy rubber mat on the other side of the scanner, you know the humiliation is just beginning. There stands a TSA masher motioning you to come closer. Once you reach Bertha, she asks you to spread your legs and arms as she menacingly tosses her electronic wand back and forth. Every muscle is seizing up as you assume the vulnerable position. (By the way, her rote preview of the assault she is about to commit— "I'm about to touch the underwire of your bra"—doesn't make the experience any less humiliating.) Then this woman who can barely bend at the waist proceeds to run her discolored rubber glove over every crevice and seam of your body. By the time you collect your things and redress yourself, you don't know whether you should head for the gate or ask for a rape kit.

In the Unlikely Event...

There is nothing more unnerving in a plane than watching a seatmate feverishly study one of those illustrated emergency cards. No normal person would do this. These dingy seat back inserts contain no words—just a series of poorly drawn comic strips depicting mayhem. Question: if the morons can't read, why should I rely on them in the event of an emergency? Shouldn't there be some explanatory text on these cards? And if they do try to follow the crude illustrations, you get the feeling that these geniuses would strangle you with one of those oxygen cords or mistake the life vest inflation tube for a Slurpee straw.

At least there is no need to fear a crash or a water evacuation. "In the unlikely event of a water landing, grab the portliest passenger to your left or right and hold on for dear life."

Safety for Dummies

For the illiterate first-time flier there is the perennial safety instruction offered by the crew before every flight. If you don't know how to snap a belt shut at this point or twist open an air vent, perhaps you should remain in the terminal. Do we really need to see the sleep-deprived flight crew go through their tired floor show before every flight?

We know: buckle the belt like this, unbuckle it like that, and pull twice on the oxygen mask, air is flowing! If I promise to do the whole routine for them as I enter the plane, can I be exempted from the safety exhibition? And some of these flight attendants get downright nasty if you don't pay attention. On a recent flight to Phoenix, one stewardess (woops) in the middle of a safety briefing noticed I was reading *The Wall Street Journal*. "Is that article on the price of gold more interesting than saving your life? Please pay attention, ma'am," she snipped. I'm sorry but your little standup isn't exactly the Rockettes' Christmas Spectacular.

Aisle Block Your Way

We need to establish a code of conduct for boarding a plane. You people who endlessly attempt to jam your huge carry-ons into the overhead compartment, trying to discern row 26 from row 27, as if you were identifying the last strand of DNA for the Human Genome project—could you please do us a favor and step *out* of the aisle? Blocking the aisle has now become a pathology that should be recognized by the DSM.

Some travelers, the moment they reach their row, feel the need to squat in the middle of the aisle and open their baggage, usually to retrieve a Mary Higgins Clark paperback or earbuds, while the rest of us stand in an unmoving line on the sweltering or freezing Jetway. This is not your private jet. Open your bag in the terminal. Retrieve your book or iPad from under your pile of unmentionables before you enter the plane, and take your seat quickly. And how about the able-bodied people who block the aisle soliciting help to hoist their bloated baggage into the overhead compartment? If you can't lift your own bag, it's time to check it at the ticket counter. Stop being so cheap.

Then there are the passengers who use the aisle to disrobe before the flight. These mostly collegiate females are known for wearing pajamas with several layers of sweaters and coats. They peel away each layer of the clothing and stuff it into the over-head before takeoff. This process usually takes several minutes and involves assistance from an eager male traveling companion. My message to these ladies: leave the sleepwear at home, and if you must travel dressed as a bum, consider the bus. On second thought, they have aisles that should be kept clear, as well. Why don't you just stay home in bed.

The Incredible Shrinking Overhead Compartment

The passengers aren't always to blame. There is no image more tragic than a grown man using all of his weight to cram a standard-size carry-on into the overhead compartments. While airlines have raised the rates for checked luggage, they have si-multaneously reduced the size of the overhead compartments. My purse can barely fit in the overhead at this point. If I include a bottle of hand sanitizer and a lipstick—it's under the seat in front of me. The new overhead compartments are angled so that they are wider at the top and come to a point at the bottom. This discourages us from placing anything larger than a binder in the darn things. The door is raked at a hard angle to ensure that the contents will spill out on anyone unfortunate enough to pull the latch. The carry-ons are like spring-loaded snakes in a peanut can.

During a recent flight I barely squeezed my roller bag into the overhead and locked the door before it tumbled out. As a courtesy, I warned the invaders coming down the aisle: "that one is full." Most of them heeded my warning, dragging their bloated backpacks, duty-free sacks, and enormous rolling cargo containers behind them down the aisle. Then a defiant man, ignoring my cautionary pleas (or maybe he just didn't speak English), reached up and began yanking on *my* latch. I resorted to waving my hands and talking the way people do when they are not dealing with a native speaker.

"Don't open. It is totally full. You will get hurt," I said, wildly gesticulating. The door popped open. My hanging bag and someone else's smaller carry-on, filled with what seemed to be dumbbells, hit the man on the head. He collapsed to the floor, blocking the aisle and delaying the flight departure by twenty minutes. The flight attendant then asked *me* to check my bag, as if I had done something wrong. "Sure, as long as we can store Mr. Hematoma in the overhead instead."

Honey, I Shrunk the Seats

As passengers expand, the seats on planes seem to be contracting. According to SeatGuru.com, Northwest Airlines has the snuggest seats in the air at only sixteen inches across. That size seat is fine if you are of normal weight, but for 60% of Americans who are overweight this just won't do. With my luck, I am usually seated next to the *Biggest Loser* contestants—before they go on the show. These are the people who lift the armrests up to make it easier for them to ooze into the adjoining seats.

If the airlines are going to shrink the seats, armrests should be immovable. They need to be part of the permanent architecture of the seat, to prevent any and all passenger "spillage." I'm not saying overweight people should have to pay more for their seats, only that they should be restricted to their own section—a place where there are no armrests; sort of a bench seat with lots of belt extensions.

Food Court in the Sky

What brain surgeon decided that people who paid hundreds of dollars to sit in a germ-filled tube at thirty thousand feet do not need food? Even in prison, you get bread and water. You know it's bad when you start considering a cup of water a perk. The airlines have had money troubles for years, so they had to make up the shortfall somewhere. In a perversely exploitative move, they began hawking expensive boxes of junk we used to get for free. In what way are these skies friendly? For $7.49, they actually charge people for a box full of miniature promotional samples. Inside are tiny bags of Goldfish, animal crackers, mini pretzels, and exactly one Keebler cookie. But no matter how hungry you are, don't you dare try to pay in cash. Only credit cards are accepted by these food hucksters.

It's only a matter of time before the airlines start charging for other formerly gratis services. If we don't stop this high-flying nickel-and-diming, we'll soon be paying a buck fifty each time we flush the onboard toilet—and another fifty cents if we want paper.

The Bring-Your-Own-Grub Crowd

With the scant "in flight" offerings, travelers have taken to bringing their own grub on board. Their culinary choices get more exotic every day. For some reason, I am always seated in the vicinity of the man who just cleaned out some garlic-themed ethnic buffet. Ingraham Flying Rule of Thumb: If the food stinks under the heat lamp, it's not going to smell any better seeping from your pores at cruising altitude. On one cross-country flight, the bald sweaty mess sitting next to me was perspiring so profusely that from his scent alone, I could not only identify the type of curried chicken he'd eaten, but also the flavor of the naan he devoured too. I didn't think it could get worse, until he opened a fresh bag of culinary stench, midair. He then spread the malodorous feast out over the adjoining tray tables. The hand over my nose and my bugging eyes must have drawn his attention. As he scooped some stinky hummus with a chip, he froze and made eye contact. "Would you like some?" he asked. "No, thank you," I answered, with feigned politeness. Where's the oxygen mask when you need it?

I also love it when mothers bring along a picnic bag of soggy sandwiches and day-old tuna wraps for their offspring. These are the ladies who ask you to pass the fishy, cellophaned stink bombs to their children three aisles down. This way, the foul smell manages to taint not just one row, but the entire compartment. Hazmat trucks should meet these flights at their final destination.

Kickers

There must be something in my frequent-flier profile. If there is a child on board with active legs, he will without fail be seated directly behind me. Other people get sedate retirees or tired businesspeople; I always end up sitting in front of a miniature David Beckham with restless leg syndrome.

I swear, these children are performing the entire Nutcracker Suite on the back of my seat. The moment I nod off or bring a drink up to my lips—*bam!* The little bugger hits me squarely in the back of the headrest. I usually let the first head concussion pass, but after, say, the fifth contusion, I feel I must protest. When I ask the parents to still Junior and remind him that this is not karate practice, they always give me the evil eye as if I did something wrong. If your child cannot control his legs in flight, he should either be bound like a felled buck or given a sippy cup of children's Benadryl for the journey (oh, sorry, was that pulled from the market?). I'm delighted that children are flying more often, but I would prefer they keep the kickboxing tryouts to themselves—or better yet, turn sideways and let Mom and Dad see how you're progressing.

Porn in Row 23

On a recent return flight from Los Angeles, I was seated next to an unaccompanied minor, who occupied the middle seat. On the other side of the boy was an Indian man with a laptop. Once airborne, the man pops on his headphones, fires up the Dell, and proceeds to watch porn. We're not talking about R-rated fare or even a nude shot or two—we are talking about full-on pornography. People began to complain, including yours truly. After at least half an hour, the flight attendant moved in and asked the guy to turn off the porn. "I have my rights, I don't tell you what to watch," the pervert barked, ignoring the complaints. I suppose once someone is willing to view pornography in front of God, a child, and everyone else, shame is not exactly an effective pressure tactic.

Passengers aren't the only ones broadcasting inappropriate fare in the air. Airlines routinely play vile films either on the overhead monitors or on the "individual viewers" that allow a personalized entertainment experience. Owing to the privacy screen, you are not supposed to be able to see what others are watching on the seat back in front of them. This gives the airlines license to feature all manner of programming, running the gamut from sexed-up romps to bloody spectaculars to Bill Maher. During a trip overseas last year, I was trying to read my Kindle, when the man across the aisle and a few rows up began to hoot and yowl. "Yeah, oooh, oooh, stab him in the face," he yelled, rocking in his seat. "Daaaamn. He got him good!" He and others in my immediate vicinity were watching a film I later learned was titled *The Mechanic.* Anyone with the right angle (i.e., mine) could clearly see every grisly frame of this opus. In the course of two hours, on neighboring screens, I saw: two people having sex in an alley; a man shot in the head; a girl's hand shoved into an in-sink disposal; a person thrown into an oncoming car; and a fat guy repeatedly stabbed with a two-pronged blunt instrument. Now *you* try eating lasagna and pudding after that.

But I've learned my lesson. I no longer gripe about the horrors I see on nearby screens, I just dig out my own laptop, put it on Maria's lap, and play *Dora the Explorer* or *Mickey Mouse Clubhouse*—full blast. If they're going to make us suffer—turnabout is fair play.

Seatback Compartments and Tray Tables

Without gloves and a pair of tongs, I would never remove anything from a seatback compartment. To my mind, these are nothing more than miniature, in-flight landfills. All manner of human refuse will, one way or another, gravitate into that seatback pocket. I have witnessed people shove drenched Kleenex into the slot, bags of vomit, half-eaten foodstuffs, used cotton swabs, and—I am not making this up—dentures. Is it any wonder that I cringe when I see a mother putting her baby's teething toys in the seat back pocket for safekeeping? She might as well store the teethers in the rear cabin commode. It has to be more hygienic.

But the most unappetizing incident that took the cake was the mother across the aisle from me who pulled down her tray table and proceeded to diaper her baby without laying out so much as a changing mat. Imagine being the passenger gifted with that seat on the next flight? I think of this scene every time

I see someone facedown on a tray table in a vain effort to sleep. Naturally, after the mother had finished changing her child, she shoved the soiled diaper in the seatback pocket. If you don't believe me, check it out for yourself. The diaper is probably still there.

In-Flight Magazines

In-flight magazines, a.k.a. gumholders, should be forbidden on board planes. During a flight, you want to focus on where you are going, not be distracted by inane stories about the places you could be going if you had unlimited funds. Do we really need to hear about the wonders of popular tourist destinations like Seoul, Dubai, and Libya? The pages also include a story or two about U.S. cities and their major attractions—places like Memphis, Philadelphia, or Houston. Usually these are the hubs of the airline you're flying. Unless they have transported Busch Gardens or the Golden Gate Bridge into terminal C, why should I be interested? The destination puff pieces are designed to make you forget the fact that your bag is missing, you missed your last connection, and you are starving. In between these must-read stories are always ads for matchmaking services, steakhouses, and some off-color show in Vegas. As if the only people who read these things are carnivorous, gambling lonely hearts.

For you community puzzle enthusiasts, in-flight magazines are a special slice of heaven. Inside each issue, there are always plenty of smudged, nearly completed sudoku cubes and crosswords. And with each attempt at solving one of the puzzles, you get a free case of contact dermatitis. But don't worry about any of this because most of the time someone has already ripped out the brainteasers and half of that article on Austin, Texas, long before you boarded.

The best thing to do is to avoid the in-flight magazine altogether. Anyone actually reading these germ collectors either forgot to bring genuine reading material aboard or is a visitor from another country.

SkyMaul

That ratty catalog in your seatback pocket must be a real eye-opener for some people. In the air, you can find legions of travelers bent in awe over this dressed-up mail order circular. I suppose *SkyMall* is a revelation, particularly for those who've never been to Sam's or the Sharper Image. Each page is jammed with products that have little to no utility. But there must be something in that recirculated air that makes them seem indispensable. Honestly, who doesn't need an electronic head massager, gravity-defying loafers, an at-home oxygen bar, a canine genealogy kit (for only $59.99!), or a garden zombie statue for your garden?

As I watch passengers ooh and aah over the catalog's treasures, I'm always tempted to say "You know, you can find that for half price on a late-night infomercial." When they look at each other with wide eyes, exclaiming "I've never seen this before!" I just want to scream out: "Do they not have QVC on your cable system? Back on earth, they sell that useless junk twenty-four hours a day—and Joan Rivers will even tell you a joke with each purchase."

That Flight Will Be Departing— Next Wednesday

Whether you are already on board or still at the gate, proceed to airline customer service or back to the parking lot to retrieve your car, if you hear any of the following five announcements:

1. "We are experiencing a slight mechanical delay. But we are assured that a mechanic is on his way."

2. (25 minutes later) "Just to give you an update. The mechanic is here, but we are awaiting the delivery of a minor part. It shouldn't be much longer."

3. (An hour later) "Sorry to report this. But just to update you, the part we needed did arrive. That problem is fixed. But the ground just discovered that the rear toilet isn't flushing. We are awaiting another mechanic to take care of that problem. We'll update you as soon as possible."

4. "As soon as the crew arrives we will begin boarding. Their inbound flight has been delayed. We'll make another announcement when we have an update."

5. "I have some good news and some bad news. The good news is the crew is here. The bad news is they have ex-

ceeded their hours and cannot board this flight—but we have called in a backup crew."

When you hear 3, 4, or 5, the flight attendants break out the drink vouchers. Don't fall for it. Keep your wits about you and get off the plane.

Not the Hotel You Booked

You thought you'd be spending the night in Cancun, Paris, or London. No, you lucky thing, you get to spend two days and nights at the airport! Airlines cancel flights with such frequency, and are so cheap, that they routinely leave passengers stranded without so much as a food coupon. With nowhere else to go, many opt to just spend the night at the airport. Some airports have begun to install showers and rest areas with cots to accommodate the sleepovers.

Then there are the thrifty travelers who actually factor an air terminal sleepover into their itinerary. Sites like SleepinginAir ports.net and Budgettravel.com advise these cheapskates on gaming the system and squatting in their airport of choice. The sites actually rate the best and worst airports for snoozing and advise their clients to pack a "cheap inflatable pool raft or travel mattress . . . eyeshades . . . an alarm clock . . . books/magazines." Why not really make yourself at home and bring along your nightstand and your four-poster bed? I'm sorry, airports—like bus terminals and train stations—are places of transit, not a lodging option. There is nothing worse than arriving at a terminal late at night to find scores of snoring people all over the terminal floor. This is not a shantytown in Johannesburg. Have some decency and rent a room.

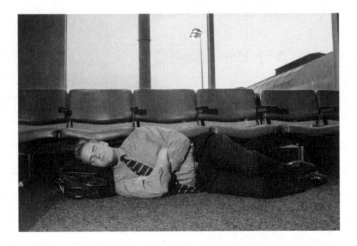

"Hey, I Just Landed!"

The last thing you want to hear after a long, uncomfortable flight is your seatmate's inane declarations into his cell phone upon touchdown. Among the not-so-greatest hits:

"Just landed." (Since cell phone use is not permitted in flight, we didn't think you were calling in midair, Orville.)

"The flight is a little late, but we're here." (Like the poor sap on the other line doesn't know that he has been circling the airport for three hours and forty-eight minutes.)

"I don't know if you can hear me, but I'm here. I can't hear you, but I'm here. I'll call you later." (If they can't hear you, why tell them you'll call later?)

Cruise Pass

Every year, I am asked to speak on a cruise, usually in the winter months. I would rather be held underwater for seven days than forced aboard one of these miserable frigates. Once you are on a cruise liner there is no escape. It's like a floating prison with ports of call. I know some people enjoy gorging themselves twenty-three times in a twenty-four-hour period, but I have better things to do than hit the mid-afternoon buffet, play shuffleboard, and attend a wine tasting seminar in the Zodiac Lounge. And as for the onboard "entertainment": I didn't like *Mama Mia!* on Broadway, I hardly think I'll enjoy it while cruising two miles off St. Thomas.

God bless "the cruisers," who for all of their sloth seem to be enjoying themselves—but when you are still able-bodied and can actually travel to sun-drenched beaches, should you really be parked in a sardine-sized cabin watching them blur by? It's like driving by an art museum and pretending that you've enjoyed the Renoirs. This kind of vicarious vacationing is just not for me. I also loathe the idea of being trapped on board a ship with people I would normally approach only while clutching a can of Mace. The salt water makes them no more sufferable.

I can tolerate a cruise for about three hours. That's enough time to check in, throw confetti as the steamer pulls away from the dock, and soak up a few rays on the Sonesta Deck. At that point I'm looking around for the helicopter to take me to shore. Perhaps when I am too infirm to move at my own will, a cruise might be a vacation option. In the meantime, if I want to unwind surrounded by water, I'll slip into a warm tub, followed by a relaxing skeet shoot off my own back deck.

Seat Hogs

The train back to D.C. was packed to capacity. Any time you leave New York on a Friday evening it's the risk you take. "Please remove your belongings from all nearby seats. We are sold out and will need every seat on this train," the announcement crackled overhead. After trudging from one car to another looking for a free spot, I finally spied one. As I got closer, it was clear that the redheaded woman in the adjoining seat had piled her coat, computer bag, and several books on the empty chair.

"Is anyone sitting here?" I asked, placing my things in the overhead.

"Yes, my friend is here. She's in the bathroom," Little Red said. Reluctantly, I pulled my bag out of the overhead and continued on to the next car, in search of a seat.

About an hour later, I made a trip to the café car and happened to pass the redhead. There on the seat next to her was the coat, the computer bag, and the untouched books arranged exactly as they were before. I stared at the seat until the woman looked up. "Where's your friend? Either she's taken a Fleet enema or she fell through the hole in the john. You'd better check on her," I said. The woman just shrugged and smiled. Liar.

Traveling Eavesdroppers

Have you ever sat on a bus or train and suddenly realized that the people across the aisle are listening to your conversation. Some are so shameless, they actually lean in for better reception. The next time this happens to you, do what I do. Walk over to Mr. or Ms. Big Ears and ask, "Would you like to sit on my lap? I don't you want you to miss anything."

The Lost Resort of Atlantis and Other Water Disasters

Have you ever seen the commercial for Atlantis, the giant Bahamas resort/waterpark? The advertising campaign makes the place look like the Taj Mahal of Caribbean luxury—gleaming castle-like hotel towers, pyramidesque water slides, and large pristine aquamarine pools. Everyone in the commercial is perfectly tanned and toned, healthy and happy. The problem is, once you get there, instead of the aquatic nirvana you were promised, you'd swear you just walked into a taping of *Jersey Shore*.

Question: if a gaggle of filthy, oily, bacteria-ridden strangers showed up at your house and asked to bathe with you, would you say yes? If not, why on earth would you ever step into a confined, shallow pool with them? And if there are tots in the water with you, run for your life. The Centers for Disease Control and Prevention reports: "A single diarrheal incident from one person could contaminate water throughout a large pool system or a waterpark." So, will the addition of a seventy-five-foot serpentine slide neutralize the uric acid and fecal matter bubbling in the current beneath you?

If you like this sort of experience, save yourself the money and install a slide into your septic tank.

Staycation

Can we banish the word "staycation" already? There is no such thing as a staycation. You either go on a vacation or you stay home. Let's not pretend that planting yourself in the La-Z-Boy and watching *American Idol* reruns is a holiday. It is not. Face it: you are a homebody who needs to immediately visit Travelocity. If you don't have the money for a vacation, there is nothing to be ashamed of. I call it being an American during the Obama recovery.

9

Holidays from Hell

There are some holidays that I'd like to rip from our national calendar and others that I wish we'd take the time to rediscover. The more you look, the more you realize that many of these special days have been created by marketers—the rest are perverted by retailers, or just ruined by visiting relatives. As much as we'd sometimes like to, there is no way to avoid holidays. Below are but a few thoughts on what distinguishes a Holi-day from a Helli-day.

New Year's Peeve

Do you feel the same sense of dread welling up in your digestive tract that I do when December 31 rolls around? It's not the passing of another year that disturbs my psyche. It's what is trotted out to usher in the new year: unfunny and awkward celebrities anchoring the New Year's coverage. The fireworks are cool, but the resolutions you'll break by February. If there is one holiday aching to be forgotten, it is New Year's Eve.

I have yet to meet a single (sober) human being who remembers having a good time on New Year's Eve. It's the turning of the Gregorian calendar. It means absolutely nothing.

When Pope Gregory XIII instituted his calendar, I can promise you that what he had in mind did not include a blinding crystal ball dropping over throngs of inebriated revelers urinating in plain sight. And I know he never contemplated anything like Ryan Seacrest. He and Dick Clark are incapable of "rockin'" a chair, much less New Year's Eve. If New York City officials really wanted to save money in these challenging economic times, they'd ditch the 2,500 lights in the Waterford Crystal Ball and just ask Ryan to stand atop Times Square and smile for 90 minutes.

What I really love are the resolutions, repeated earnestly by our friends and family members year after year. "I'm going to stop drinking during the week!" (A favorite pledge of the perpetually sloshed.) "I'm going to read a book a week!" (Oh please, the first and last book that person has ever read was the instruction manual for his Nintendo.) On New Year's Eve, I'm always standing next to the heavy-hitter with a champagne glass in one hand, a baby back rib in the other, resolving to "get fit" in the new year. Or maybe he was saying "get fat."

Groundhog Nay

How did a rodent emerging from a hole in the wee hours of the morning get his own holiday? Please don't even try to suggest that this woodchuck has any foreknowledge of the weather. If the animal sees its shadow, it supposedly means six more weeks of winter. This creature spends so much time underground, it's lucky to see anything at all in bright sunlight. Run out of the exit door of a movie theater on a sunny day and tell me what you can see. It'd be a miracle if your dilating pupils saw an oncoming Ford 150, much less your shadow.

Crowds of up to forty thousand assemble annually in Punxsutawney, Pennsylvania, in the predawn hours of February 2 to await the groundhog's big exit. And though there are other Groundhog Day celebrations, nothing quite matches the turnout for Punxsutawney Phil. There are always a gaggle of men in long black coats and top hats surrounding the burrow, creating a perfect backdrop for the *Today* show's live coverage. I love how major American media figures treat Punxsutawney Phil's emergence with the solemnity usually reserved for a state funeral. News alert, Ann! The critter's not coming out to announce a nuclear strike. He's an overfed beaver looking for his next handout.

I would be far more willing to observe Groundhog Day if it celebrated something worthwhile—like rodent control in America. Wouldn't you pay to see one of those old codgers in the top hats hit Punxsutawney Phil with a blow dart as he exited his burrow and throw him into the back of an animal control van?

We could rename it Groundhog Management Day. Considering what the critters do to gardens and home foundations, that's a holiday we could all get behind.

Valentine's Kiss-off

If there ever was a trumped-up holiday designed entirely to keep restaurateurs, florists, and card manufacturers in business, it is Valentine's Day. Rarely has a holiday been so divorced from its roots or history. It was at one time called St. Valentine's Day, established purportedly to pay tribute to the Christian martyr of the same name. One legend has it that Father Valentine, a priest, defied the Roman emperor's decree forbidding young men to marry. The emperor Claudius II believed that single guys would make better soldiers. Valentine continued to marry young couples in secret, and when he was discovered, he was martyred. He died for love and even concluded his hastily written notes with "Your Valentine." This is a sweet story, but it is probably malarkey. There is so little known about St. Valentine that Pope Paul VI officially removed him and his day from the Catholic Church's calendar of saints in 1969. Apparently, Hallmark missed the memo.

Now, Valentine's Day is just an excuse for overpriced, awkward romantic encounters. Restaurants routinely double their prices so unhappy couples can be as miserable in public as they are at home. One year, I remember sitting in an upscale French restaurant on Valentine's Day, when at the far end of the room, a couple began arguing, heatedly. Before long, they were cursing at each other. A waiter scampered over to quell the storm—to no avail. Before it was over, the woman had thrown a glass of wine at her dining companion and the maitre d' got punched in the mouth. Maybe this was an appropriate way to remember St. Valentine. After all, violent passions surfaced, and blood was spilled. Ain't love grand?

The most unsettling aspect of eating out on Valentine's Day is having to look over the landscape of nervous first-daters in the room. When you over hear the question, "So where are you from?" coming from the next table, or maybe, "Have you ever been to this restaurant before? It seems really nice," you know you're in for a show.

Lifestyle magazines now encourage men to show their sensitive side by creating their own homemade valentines for the lady in their life. May I offer this pointed suggestion: if your valentine involves disfiguring a doily with scissors or the use of crayons in any capacity, you may want to seek the help of a trained professional—and I don't mean Martha Stewart. The thought of a grown man toiling over glitter, glue, and red construction paper is not exactly a libido booster.

Even kids are obliged to participate in the Valentine madness. Each year, I have to run to the drugstore to pick up boxes of valentines for my kids to distribute to their classmates. This year, as I sat at the kitchen table helping my daughter fill them out, I suddenly thought, "Why are we encouraging our kids to send love notes to everyone in their classroom? Shouldn't we help them to be a bit more discriminating?" The whole point of Valentine's Day is to give something special to someone who is special to you. Once you give something to everyone in the class, doesn't it negate the entire purpose? Maybe we should have the kids write one global valentine to post on the main school bulletin board: "Won't you ALL be my Valentine?"

Unpresidential Day

At one time it was the only national holiday to honor a single American, the father of our country, George Washington. Over time, and due to the proximity of Abraham Lincoln's Birthday, Congress decided to move Washington's Birthday to the third Monday of February. Big problem: it never falls on Washington's actual birthday, February 22. But never mind, the day has now unofficially become Presidents' Day, a national moment when we remember not only the father of our country and Lincoln, but great leaders like Millard Filmore and Barack Obama. If we were honest about what this day really represents to most Americans, we'd rename it something simple, like February Ski Day.

It is offensive to the memory of Washington to turn his birthday (still the official reason for Presidents' Day) into a generic catchall for every man who ever held the office. I realize it's an opportunity to reflect on the legacies of outstanding men like Reagan and Roosevelt, but it also brings to mind others whom we are still trying to purge from our national memory.

Just because a man has occupied the Oval Office does not mean that the whole nation should have to stop and think about him once a year. Be honest, do you get the warm fuzzies when thinking of Chester A. Arthur and Rutherford B. Hayes? And I doubt if Carter and Nixon are foremost in the minds of Americans as they observe Presidents' Day (though I admit the Planter's Peanut shell costumes and plumber uniforms would make for exciting and educational celebrations). Personally, I am holding out for Impeached Presidents Day. Andrew Johnson and Bill Clinton are crying out to be remembered. Can you imagine the special holiday parades organized in their honor? Confederate flags and thongs as far as the eye can see.

St. Patrick's Day

Never has a saint been so maligned in all of history. Poor St. Patrick brought the Christian faith to the Irish and drove the snakes and the Druids from their isle, and all he got for it was a global excuse to drink.

The religious example of the saint and his bold spiritual leadership have been all but lost on St. Patrick's Day. Today, all that remains is an orgy of people wearing green plastic hats, up-chucking in the street. Where his followers once crammed into churches, they now squeeze into stinky pubs, fighting over pints of green Guinness. Ingraham Rule of Thumb: Beware of entering any eating establishment with the word "Irish" in the title. The food served comes in only two forms—"mash" or "pot pies." And usually the "mash" is just what's in the "pot pie." In fact, the pies usually taste as though they were cooked in a pot—a chamber pot. And what about that stale stench of the floors in these joints? Hey, Mr. Lucky Charms, that's not a pot of gold at the end of that rainbow, it's a bucket of vomit.

At least shamrocks are still widely displayed—even if they are made by child laborers in Sichuan Province. Legend tells us St. Patrick used the three-leaf clover to teach people about the Trinity. Unfortunately, most of modern society has no concept of the Trinity and hasn't seen a shamrock outside of a cereal bowl. More than fifteen hundred years after his death, I suppose it's good that people still remember Patrick's name. Though when your name is synonymous with green fountains and the Celtic Woman tour—being forgotten has its advantages.

April Fools Me Once . . .

April Fools' Day—finally, a holiday with a wide and growing constituency. We should convene an annual competition to crown a national April Fool. There would certainly be no lack of competition. The morning shows could do live coverage from outside the winner's home. If somebody like, say, Nancy Pelosi sees her shadow as she exits the dwelling, it means twelve more months of her stupidity. If she doesn't see her shadow, she becomes an instant contestant on *Wipeout*, after which she promises to leave the national stage. Wouldn't that be fun?

April Fools' Day is one of those harmless and, dare I say,

therapeutic holidays. Though unofficial, it is twenty-four hours of pranks and unexpected gags. On April first, 2010, I went on air and for a full hour renounced every political position and principle I have ever held. "I've been thinking: this whole liberty thing is very overrated," I said. "Somebody needs to step in and fix this country. I feel blessed that this administration and this Congress are leading—laying down new regulations for our citizenry and private industry. Yes, we need more government control in our lives; more taxes to distribute the wealth, and much less of this hypocritical God talk. It's so judgmental. The change we needed has arrived—and it is change we can truly believe in." The audience went crazy. The lines were lit up all morning with stunned callers. I decided to keep the gag going by arguing with each listener who disagreed with my newfound take on the issues. Posing as a liberal is really easy, you just have to emote while repeating the same hackneyed lines about "social justice" and "green jobs" and the "brilliance" of Barack Obama's oratory.

Un-Earthed Day

For those with scant-to-no religious faith, there is a high holy day set aside for them to worship the ground, if nothing else. Earth Day was founded by a politician, Senator Gaylord Nelson of Wisconsin, in 1970, to create a protest that would hasten passage of new environmental laws. It spawned a new greeniac movement that would change everything from the types of lightbulbs we use to the water flow in our toilet bowls.

The Earth Day worshippers were smart. They knew that if they could win over young converts, their loopy agenda would be adopted by the broader public. So now school children have been frightened into celebrating this pagan holiday. A friend of mine with children in public and private schools recently shared their Earth Day projects with me. In one, the kids had to color a picture of a sad, sickly planet earth, and then draw sketches depicting all the horrible things humans do to make "her sick." (How is a child supposed to sketch "Maury" Povich, Rev. Al Sharpton, and "Chaz" Bono?) So not only are we teaching kids to venerate the earth, but we're also forcing them to believe that human beings are toxic to the planet. In another project, an older child at a religious school had to make a list of all the "sins we commit against the earth." It's good to know that sin is still a reality, but I didn't realize dropping a bubble gum wrapper on the lawn is now on the same spiritual plane as beheading.

The National Mall has become the Mecca of the Earth Day silliness. What decades ago was a one-day "teach-in" on April 22 has metastasized into a weeklong green freak show. Useless outdoor events fill the week, attended by people who either are unemployed or should be. The Earth Day Climate Rally is the apex of the gathering. In 2010, it featured performers like Sting, John Legend, the Roots, and others spreading the gospel of green. (Hey, Sting, did you kayak across the Atlantic to get there or hop the G-5?) Protestors wandered around the Mall dressed as the blue people from *Avatar* while union leaders and Jesse Jackson yelled into microphones. After seeing some of the folks who turn out for these Earth Day activities, I have a question: is it really worth saving the planet if everyone on it is this filthy? Are deodorant and soap now on the green "do not buy" list? And don't give me the bit about how you use only "sustainable" soaps made of "vegetable oil." Bottom line: When you slip into that hemp clothing, you smell like a three-day-old fish fry.

The holy sacrament of Earth Day has become an excuse to agitate for a cap-and-trade bill: an environmental pet project that will tax carbon emissions, kill jobs, and drive up energy costs. It died in the last Congress and won't get anywhere in the new one. But maybe in the *Avatar* sequel, James Cameron can get cap and trade passed on Pandora.

The Easter Hunt

When Easter rolls around, it's not only the eggs you have to hunt for, but Easter itself. Remember when Easter was a holy day? For more than two thousand years, it has commemorated the resurrection of Jesus Christ. Now you'd think that when Jesus returned from the dead, he was pursued not by Peter the Apostle but by Peter the RABBIT, followed by ten pink Peeps.

Now, I love chocolate eggs as much as the next diabetic, but we already have one annoying holiday dedicated to the distribution and consumption of candy. Must we mar a sacred holiday as well? It's one thing to give the kids a basket of goodies, but now Easter has turned into a second Christmas, with the Easter

Bunny delivering not just candy, but toys, too! Only this time, they aren't placed under a plastic tree, they're buried in plastic grass. (Which must be made by the vacuum manufacturers, because that stuff is impossible to pick up.)

And can we please give the Easter Bunny at the mall a rest? Putting a teenager in a dirty bunny costume (which never fits correctly—the head is always off kilter) will not draw people to your lousy mall! An overgrown mammal staring at you as you buy shoes is never comforting. Children being paraded up to the Easter Bunny staging area always have the same look of horror on their little faces. None of them believe, even for a moment, that that fetid furry-headed rabbit is real. Shopping malls need to accept the facts: Easter is not the buying season that Christmas is, and no matter how many gargantuan hares you situate near Macy's, we're not buying any more of your stuff. Let's put the mall bunnies in the tomb for three days and see what happens.

Hallmark Holidays

I am one of those mothers who love to awaken to a sweet bouquet of spring flowers and a card on Mother's Day. I'm sure millions of moms share my sentiments. Fathers probably feel the same way about the day designated to honor them. So while I will defend Father's Day and Mother's Day, that's where I draw the line. In recent years, a host of auxiliary days have mysteriously cropped up. They serve no other purpose except to pressure us into spending our hard-earned money on chintzy cards. They either bear trite, disingenuous sentiments or blare bad, cheesy music upon opening—would '80s hair bands have any resonance in the modern culture were it not for these unwanted thirty-second interludes?

Here are some of the more notorious examples of "Hallmark Holidays":

- *National Doctor's Day* (March 30): Shouldn't insurance cover the price of this card? And why not be more specific? "Glad to know you're always there behind me! Happy Proctologist's Day!"
- *Secretary's Day* (April 27): Now called Administrative Professionals Day; secretaries, receptionists, and other support staff are treated to goodies and time off. Sounds like a shakedown to me. Give them another few years, and it'll be called Executive Enabler Day or The People Who Really Do All the Work Day.
- *National Nurses Day* (May 6): Do we even have enough nurses left in America to properly celebrate this day?
- *Parents' Day* (fourth Sunday in July): Yet another milestone achieved by Bill Clinton, who formally signed this day into law in 1994. When I think of good parenting, I always think of Bill Clinton. Question: Once we send you a card on Mother's Day or Father's Day, isn't that

sufficient? Forget the parent trap, we're caught in the card trap.

- *Sisters' Day* (first Sunday in August): Where does it end? What about Nieces' Day, Half-Brother Day, Second Cousin Once Removed Day, and That-Weird-Guy-Who-Shows-Up-Each-Thanksgiving-Who-May-or-May-Not-Be-Vaguely-Related-To-Us Day?

- *Friendship Day* (first Sunday in August): Since it occupies the same spot on the calendar as Sisters' Day, this must be a backstop celebration for those who lack female siblings. Aside from the Hallmark website, you would be hard pressed to find anyone who has ever heard of, much less celebrated, this stupid day.

- *Grandparents Day* (Sunday after Labor Day): Last time I checked you were still mothers and fathers, right? You've already had your day. No more cards, Gramps.

- *Clergy Appreciation Day* (first Sunday in October): Another gift from our friends at Hallmark. It's too bad that I'm always busy this day each year celebrating Churchgoer Appreciation Day. My pastor hasn't caught on yet.

- *National Boss Day* (October 16): It's not enough to ask "how high" every time he says "jump"; now you have to buy the guy a card. Like Churchgoer Appreciation Day, the celebration is not widespread, though Hallmark has been making cards for this holiday since 1979—their optimism is inspiring. Still, I must say, it's curious that while I have employed dozens of staff over the years, I have yet to be recognized with a card on October 16. Hmmmmm.

Take Our Daughters and Sons to Work Day

Unless you work at a school or a correctional facility, please don't!

Patriotic Holidays

There is a string of uniquely American holidays that we should not only celebrate, but teach our children to respect. Memorial Day marks the start of the summer holidays and has morphed into a day of cookouts and beach parties. The last Monday of May was not reserved as a federal holiday so you could have some extra time to get bombed and tanned. The intention was to honor the men and women of the U.S. military who gave their lives in the service of the country. It is a solemn day of remembrance, not a day for buying marked-down refrigerators or body surfing. Put down the Miller Lite Longneck for a moment and go to a national cemetery. Honor those who gave you the freedom to ignore a sacred day.

Veterans Day is commemorated on November 11, and honors the millions of Americans who have served in our armed forces. It should be a national expression of gratitude to these brave men and women. Instead, it has become a day to take advantage of the blowout sales at Best Buy. Unless you're buying a laptop for a needy veteran or the *Band of Brothers* box set, it seems disrespectful.

Along with Flag Day and Independence Day (we should call it this, not "the Fourth of July"), we have neglected these essential national holidays, allowing them to become breaks without meaning. Isn't it sad that while we enjoy the benefits of freedom, we never take the time to reflect on how difficult it was to attain, or how we plan to keep it? Memorial Day, Veterans Day, Flag Day, Independence Day—each of these speaks to our national unity, our sense of purpose, our identity as a people. Our failure to fully celebrate these occasions and teach our children what they mean will only in time distance us as Americans, and unravel the fragile bonds that hold us together as a nation. So use the next American holiday, as a family, to learn more about your country and to appreciate the many gifts that she has given us. You can even light a sparkler or two, if it makes you feel good. (Aren't I a generous spirit?)

Trick or Train Wreck

Halloween is absolutely the most terrifying night of the year. When else do we unquestioningly open our door to strangers? While most of the time it's just cute kids shaking their trick-or-treat bags for a few Mounds bars, there is a new variety of trick-or-treater that is downright scary. When I spy them approaching my door, I always grab the candy bowl with the Taser in it.

Is there anything more unnerving than fully grown teens, and at times adults, posing as trick-or-treaters? There really should be a national age limit. I feel like telling them, "Go buy your own candy."

When you open the door and the "kids" are a foot taller than you are—it is time for them to stop trick-or-treating. When they have facial hair, a girlfriend, and a baby in their arms—it's time for them to stop trick-or-treating. When they drive up, park, and leave their car idling in your driveway—it is time for them to stop trick-or-treating. When they say "Trick or treat" with a voice deeper than Janet Napolitano's, it is time for them to stop trick or treating. And if they pilot themselves to your front door on a Rascal with an AARP sticker on the back, they absolutely should stop trick-or-treating.

I'd almost be willing to hand the candy over to them if they took some pride in their costumes. But year after year, I get the same enormous teenager in a ripped-up T-shirt with his mom's black eye shadow surrounding his eyes.

"What are you supposed to be?" I asked the kid one year.

He looked bewildered, turned to his friends, and laughed. "Trick or treat," he said.

"I assume you are in costume. So what are you supposed to be—I mean, other than a surly surging pile of adolescent hormones?" I pressed.

"It doesn't matter . . . I'm a zombie kind of thing."

"Oh yeah," I said. "Well, I'm dressed as a miser kind of thing this year," and I slammed the door in his face. The hooligans later egged my house, but the point stands: if you are going to take the time to extort candy from people all evening, have the decency to wear a real costume. We need something to distract us from your size and advanced age.

I will admit that today's trick-or-treaters don't have it easy. Have you taken a look at the size of the candy being offered at some of these houses? Miniatures—sawed-off, tiny bite-size versions of favorite candies—have become all the rage. Why not just hand out individual raisins? If you can't give the kiddies a normal candy bar—just turn off your house lights and hide in the dark, cheapskate.

Then there are the people who try to get all artsy with their

Halloween treats. Your kid goes up to their door and comes away with a pencil and a nickel. What is this, the Great Depression? The kid can't even buy a miniature with a nickel. One house last year gave each of my kids exactly two peanuts. And don't you love the people who stand on their front porch policing the candy bowl. "Just take one. Only one per customer," they bark out. Why not bend your big butt over and dole the candy out yourself? Don't expect the kids to be as tight as you are. Then again, maybe the Halloween porch police are on to something. A few years ago, I filled a big silver punch bowl with candy (full-sized candy, I might add). When I got home, not only was all the candy gone, but so was my sterling silver bowl. I just know it was that "zombie kind of thing" driving the Chevy Malibu.

Butter Bawling Turkey?

Several years ago, some friends in a major metropolitan city (that shall remain nameless) invited me to Thanksgiving dinner at their apartment. From the moment I arrived, all they could talk about was the "fresh organic turkey" we would soon feast upon. "It's important to me that the bird was free, living freely before we purchased him. I think you'll taste the difference," my friend enthused. Frankly, whether the bird was in a freezer at the corner market or fluttering around in a field a few days ago makes zero difference to me.

But, after consuming one of these organic birds, I can report: there is a huge difference. The frozen Butterball tastes like a turkey. The organic thing tastes like burnt seagull. It was like eating a warm wood chip. I have since discovered that the taste was attributable to the fact that most of the organic birds are not pre-basted, so the natural juices just race out of the meat. Oh, and my friend will be very sad to learn that the organic turkey that he paid eight bucks a pound for might not have been a free-range bird after all. An organic bird is not necessarily a free-roaming bird.

Others have forsaken the Thanksgiving turkey altogether. The vegans among us have made a recent habit of serving a "Tofurkey" on the big day. They take slabs of tofu, shove it into a blender, throw in some herbs, and let it dry overnight into a mold. Anything that has the consistency of curds is not likely to resemble a turkey when it comes out of the oven. It looks more like a smoking, spongy brown helmet. Imagine toasted Spam surrounded by cranberries and you're getting warmer. I only tried it once, but eating turkey droppings could not be more disgusting than that "Tofurkey." Until soy starts to gobble, it will never again cross these lips at Thanksgiving.

Christmas in October

Every year, it seems Christmas arrives earlier and earlier. We barely have the Halloween decorations up and suddenly it's time to start Jingle Belling. Why not just deck the halls in shamrocks and start the Christmas celebrations in March? At least you've got half the color scheme in place.

Last year, I walked into a store to get school supplies for my children and the clerks were already loading the shelves with Christmas garlands, lights, and wrapping paper. Going to a mall any time after Labor Day is like Alice falling through a Yuletide looking glass. No matter what the calendar says, snow is falling and reindeer are invading.

Even radio stations start playing Christmas tunes the day after Halloween. I love Christmas music, but do any of us need two months of that grating "Feliz Navidad"? What happened to Thanksgiving? Aside from Macy's parade (which is really just a way to usher in the Christmas buying season), Thanksgiving has been practically forgotten. It has been edged out by the wider culture, because the only things to sell you at Thanksgiving are turkeys, hams, pumpkin pies, and Pepto Bismol.

The early Christmas trappings are about one thing: selling junk. Christmastime is a retailer's salvation; the season when they sell more product in two months than the rest of the year combined. They naturally want to extend it for as long as possible. But when Santa and the elves start showing up in late summer, we have a problem. Now Rudolph doesn't have to worry about guiding Santa through a snowstorm, he has to worry about getting sun poisoning!

There may be only one way to keep Santa from arriving months in advance: don't buy any Christmas loot until after Thanksgiving. The stores will eventually get the message. Otherwise, we might soon find ourselves putting sparklers on the Christmas tree—in July!

Recycled Presents

The Christmas luncheon was going so well. The conversation was easy, the drinks were good, and the meal was superb. Then it came time to exchange gifts. All the women at the luncheon turned their attention to each lady as she opened her gift. A glittering green box with a bow was finally passed to me. I knew it was from my friend, whom I will call Kathy. I pried off the ribbon, tore away the paper, and there in the box was the vase that I had given Kathy as a birthday present earlier that year. If you are going to regift an item, please make sure you don't give it back to the person who gave it to you in the first place.

Whether the bad economy is to blame or just plain old cheapness, regifting is on the rise. One Christmas, someone gave me a silver serving tray. It was contemporary and really elegant. As I opened it, the gift giver went on and on about how much time she had spent searching for the ideal tray. She claimed the moment she laid eyes on it she thought, "This is Laura." I thanked her effusively. A few weeks later, when I was cleaning the tray after a party, I noticed the touching inscription on the underside of the tray: "To Jane, I'm always here to serve. . . . Your 'Hotness.'" Since I have never gone by Jane and don't know anyone called 'Hotness,' I kind of figured that the tray was not purchased for me. It's one thing to recycle a gift card or a candle, but could we at least take the time to check the item for personal inscriptions?

The worst type of presents are what I call regurgi-gifts. These are items that are so undesirable that they have been regifted more than once, sometimes boomeranging around the country, even the world, back to the original gift giver. You see regurgi- gifts making the rounds at offices a lot. A secretary gets a Snug- gie from someone down the hall and later throws it in a gift bag at the last minute for the Secret Santa party. A receptionist now gets the Snuggie and, knowing she has four at home, decides to regift it to that sweet woman on the third floor—the same sweet woman who bought the Snuggie at the Walgreens in the first place. The old saying is true: what goes around, comes around . . . especially when it's crap.

Holiday Gear

Holiday-themed clothing is not an acceptable fashion choice, ever. You know what I am talking about, and you know who you are. Some examples:

- Felt antlers on adults in the workplace.
- Sweatshirts with appliqué snowmen, reindeer, pumpkins, shamrocks, turkeys, the Easter Bunny, candy canes, or Santa.
- Brooches that light up and play Christmas tunes.
- Candy-striped socks, caps, or stockings. Also, pumpkin socks, caps, or stockings.
- Any clothing involving spangles, rhinestones, or sequins that spell out "Happy Halloween" or "Ho Ho Ho." Who do you think you are, Dolly Parton? Spare us your holiday sparkle and just send a sensible card.

Unseasoned Greetings

How I used to love receiving Christmas cards. No more. Because I know what lurks within those red envelopes: Yuletide narcissism and information that I really don't care to know.

People today feature only what's really important on their Christmas cards: pictures of themselves on sun-kissed beaches or other exotic locales. There was no room at the inn for Joseph and the Virgin Mary and apparently no room on the card either. The closest these people come to a Virgin is their connecting Virgin Atlantic flight to Bali. When did Christmas become the time to brag about the past year's luxury vacations? Let's face it—these cards are not meant to bring joy into the heart of their recipients. They are designed to do one thing—engender envy and resentment. While you were toiling at your boring desk job all year, these jerks were parasailing in Bermuda. "Merry, Merry, Suckers!"

Another favorite Christmas card cover is the family in matching sweaters seated in the backyard. What are we to make of this? Did Target have a closeout on ugly red reindeer sweaters? Or did you all just happen to dress ridiculously at the same moment and run out into the yard? Is this a Christmas card or an L.L. Bean catalog?

Perhaps most offensive is the annual Christmas letter that some feel compelled to include with their cards. You open the envelope and out falls what looks like a Xeroxed ransom note. Please keep your annual family narrative out of the Christmas card. We don't care that you and the kids scaled a mountain in Nepal or your cockapoo had hip surgery back in October. I barely have time to read my kids' report cards, much less your grammatically challenged, single-spaced reflections on the year gone by. If I should suddenly desire inarticulate remembrances, I'll go buy a Jimmy Carter memoir—or maybe check out what the Unabomber is writing these days in prison. The only card I would care to receive from these self-promoting people at Christmas is a lotto scratch-off. At least then I might win something that I could donate to charity.

The most insulting greeting of the season is the e-Christmas card. These free cards are packed with low-rent animation of horses trudging through the snow or Santa kicking back by the fire, usually ending with a dopey sign-off. "Season's Greetings from your friends the Shellys." (Which season are they speaking of—duck hunting season?) From December through the New Year, my email is always loaded with these e-cards. They require you to click on a link to retrieve your personalized "greeting"— which I usually ignore. My feeling is, if you can't be bothered to sign your name and lick a stamp, why should I expend energy and time to click on a link?

Not only is the e-card unsatisfactory as a greeting, but if you don't click the link it harasses you with repeated reminders. Suddenly the greeting card has turned into your own personal stalker. If Hallmark is for those who care enough to send the very best, the e-card is for those who just don't care at all—but had to do something since they'd already received your card in the mail.

10

Eat, Pray . . . Just Keep God Out of It

Faith is a gift—and apparently there are a lot of Americans in the returns line. There is a hostility toward religious faith today that didn't exist thirty or forty years ago—a creeping secularism that is attempting to push religion to the margins of the culture. The religiphobes have done a bang-up job. From portraying people of faith as idiots and Koran burners to casting all clergy as pedophiles and money grubbers, the seculars have done their worst. I have news for them: if wacky sermons, off-kilter fashion, and scandalous behavior haven't killed religion after all these centuries, what chance does Richard Dawkins have?

The root of a culture, as the word implies, is "cult," that which a people worship or venerate. This devotion colors and shapes society. Western civilization from its arts to its ethics to its law has been profoundly influenced by Judeo-Christian religious belief—and even today that heritage undergirds the American experiment. It has given us strength, wisdom, inspiration, and in our time, some of the worst music of any single institution in history. Contemporary church music rivals Ke$ha and Lil'Wayne on the Ingraham iPod Do Not Play list. Still, off-key and all, I'd put religion up against the seculars for durability and staying power any day. After the fads and foolishness of today are long forgotten, this is the stuff that perseveres and endures. Amen.

Spiritual but Not Religious

It has become the default response of spiritual inquiry. Ask a cosmopolitan friend or a young person to describe his or her religion and you are likely to get "I'm spiritual but not religious." Prepare to hear the line more often in the future.

A 2009 survey by LifeWay Christian Resources found that 72 percent of millennials (i.e., eighteen to twenty-nine years old) claimed to be "more spiritual than religious." A *Newsweek* poll that same year revealed that 30 percent of Americans considered themselves "spiritual but not religious." Either Oprah Winfrey has a lot of fans or these people have a commitment problem. It's like telling a spouse "I love you, but I'm not passionate." Odds are, they really don't love you that much.

Whatever its logical failings, the "spiritual but not religious" moniker has become so trendy, it now has its own acronym: S-B-N-R. How about this one: S-T-U-P-I-D? The SBNR crowd is caught in spiritual limbo. Its adherents reject organized religion (as if God or His designs are disorganized), opting to create their own mix and match religious experience. Sort of like Madonna at a Presbyterian Bible Study.

I once knew an Ivy League–educated woman, a writer, who simultaneously studied the Koran, practiced Transcendental Meditation, and would occasionally frequent a Pentecostal church because she enjoyed "the fellowship." After consorting with the Muslims and Buddhists, it's a wonder she had time for any more fellowship. Perpetually dipping their hands into the Whitman Sampler of Faith, these searchers taste each flavor, but never stay long enough to savor any one in particular. In the end, the "spiritual but not religious" label becomes the refuge of the non-committed. They usually end up, in the words of Joseph Campbell, "following their bliss" to Secularville.

There is also an antireligious bent among "the spiritual but not religious" community. They truly believe all religions are simply different versions of the same myth. The website SBNR.org offers this endearing catchphrase: "All religions contain some wisdom, but no religion contains all wisdom." One thing's for sure, the SBNR.org website contains no wisdom at all. Among its offerings is an animated yogi teaching meditation, and daily "Spirituality News and Posts" selected to reinforce people in their doubt. How tolerant and peaceful.

"I don't need to define myself to any community by putting myself in a box labeled Baptist, or Catholic, or Muslim," Heather Cariou, a self-described "spiritual instead of religious" author, told CNN. "When I die, I believe all my accounting will be done to God, and that when I enter the eternal realm, I will not walk though a door with a label on it." Sister, look more closely, there is a sign, it says idiots enter here.

If the SBNR folks were truly "spiritual," they would by nature be religious. To be spiritual is to recognize that you have a soul, a spirit—and the highest aspiration of a soul is the love of God, and reverence for Him. Last time I checked, that's called religion. What many of these spiritual searchers reject are the obligations of loving God as defined by established faith traditions. Whatever faith one chooses, it requires a full embrace of certain eternal truths and credos—a humility that recognizes you are not God and that He is. In the Christian faith that means baptism and full communion—learning the deposit of faith left by the Apostles, and conducting one's life in accordance with those Truths. A religious tradition can be truly experienced only by full participation. To live otherwise is not being spiritual, but being Deepak Chopra.

Based on my own experiences with the SBNR crowd, I think the entire movement needs to be renamed. SBNR, spiritual but not really.

The Orthodox Atheists

When did atheists become so evangelical? I mean, if you don't believe something to be true, wouldn't you just ignore it? That's certainly what I do. Whether it's leprechauns or a congressional debt reduction plan—if I'm convinced it's fiction, I simply put it out of my mind. Not the atheists. They are obsessed with faith and religious practice. Their identities and their works are one big reaction to that which they hate. No longer content to simply dismiss God and those who follow in Him, the New Atheists have created a cult of unbelief. You haven't seen dogma until you've encountered some of these atheists in full evangelical mode. They don't just mean to disparage the faithful—they want converts. And their recent efforts have borne some fruit.

The number of self-declared atheists is at an all-time high, according to the latest American Religious Identification survey, conducted by the U.S. Census Bureau. In 2001 there were 900,000 atheists; today there are 1.6 million. And do you know what the fastest-growing religion in the United States is? No religion. Gallup reports that 16 percent of Americans claim to have no religious identity—another all-time high.

None of this is surprising. Richard Dawkins, the author of *The God Delusion,* and other new atheists like Sam Harris and Christopher Hitchens have made impressive inroads into the pop culture. Their bestselling books have spawned an aggressive approach toward religion that challenges belief at every turn. While Christians are intimidated into hiding their faith under a bushel, the atheists are out of the closet in force. Last Christmas a group called American Atheists placed a cheeky billboard near the Lincoln Tunnel in New Jersey that read "You KNOW it's a myth. This season, celebrate REASON." Meanwhile the American Humanist Association launched a series of TV ads that portrayed religious texts as promoting "fear, hatred, and intolerance" while celebrating the "love" and "freedom" embodied in secularist writings. On Capitol Hill, the atheists lobbied Representative Pete Stark to introduce a resolution to declare February 12 national Darwin Day. The measure would affirm "the validity of Darwin's theory of evolution by natural selection." Christmas envy, anyone? I guess atheists want to celebrate their patron saint on an observed holy day as well—good luck with that.

Even the military is not immune from the atheist advances. According to the Associated Press, a small band of sixty-five atheists at Fort Bragg want the army to officially recognize them as a "distinct faith group." Oh, I get it now: the absence of faith suddenly qualifies them to be an official faith community. You see, atheism has become a religion after all. Though they may have a retention problem.

If people don't believe in God, it's pretty hard to get them to place their belief in a nonbelieving organization. Only 675 people registered to attend the 2011 American Atheists annual convention in Iowa, according to the *Des Moines Register*. But that didn't stop the group from covering buses all over town with the ad: "You KNOW there is NO GOD! We Know You're Right." Time will tell.

Two thousand years from now, we'll see if anybody is still reading Richard Dawkins. And when one of these atheists suddenly rises from the dead, be sure to drop me a line.

Unholy Week

Each Easter, it's more predictable than the dyed eggs, and the big bunny. Secularists always choose Holy Week, the most sacred time in the Christian calendar, to attack, degrade, and besmirch Christianity and its cherished beliefs. A few years ago, a so-called New York artist created an anatomically correct, edible, chocolate Jesus for Holy Week. *Newsweek*'s Easter edition in 2009 declared "The Decline and Fall of Christian America;" and sensational books like *The Jesus Papers: Exposing the Greatest Cover-up in History* claimed that Jesus had a wife and kids. The Easter treats for Christians just go on and on.

On Easter 2011, Lady Gaga blessed the holy day with the release of her inspirational single, "Judas." Dressed as a Goth Mary Magdalene in the video, Gaga sings to accompaniment that sounds like every other Lady Gaga song: "Jesus is my virtue, and Judas is the demon I cling to ... I'm just a holy fool ... but I'm still in love with Judas, baby." The teachers at the Convent of the Sacred Heart must be very proud of their little alumna.

On Good Friday, James Frey, the author who got into all kinds of hot water for fabricating his supposed memoir, *A Million Little Pieces,* released a new book, titled *The Final Testament of the Holy Bible.* The book details the Lord's second coming. In this work of creative genius, Jesus is a recovering alcoholic, living in a dirty Bronx apartment, who impregnates prostitutes for kicks. Naturally, Oprah (who famously outed Frey for making up stories in his memoir) invited him back to push his anti-Christian tract before her syndicated show went off the air.

Each Easter, filmmaker Simcha Jacobovici can always be relied on to make an appearance. A few Easters ago, he claimed to have discovered Jesus's family tomb, including an ossuary containing the remains of Jesus. On Easter 2011, he unveiled a new discovery: that's right, Jacobovici had found the nails of Jesus's crucifixion. The world yawned. A small query: assuming he found Jesus's remains years ago—which totally undermined the resurrection and Christ's ascension to heaven—why should we care about the crucifixion nails that were used to kill Him? Following the filmmaker's reasoning, Jesus would be a fraud. Jacobovici should know all about frauds.

Note to two-bit filmmaker: Jesus's crucifixion nails have been on display in Rome's Basilica of the Holy Cross in Jerusalem since 325. Tradition tells us that Constantine's mother, St. Helena, discovered the relics in the Holy Land and brought them back to Rome, where a church was built to house them. Jacobovici is just another religious huckster who preys on the public's historical ignorance, creating sensational events around nothing (not one archaeologist would vouch for his nail discovery). He even admitted to Bloomberg News, "Do I know 100 percent that these nails were used to crucify Jesus? No, I think we have a very compelling case to say: these are them." That didn't stop the History Channel from airing a special on this non-find. Maybe we can send out a team of archaeologists to see if they can recover

Jacobovici's credibility. I think he left it somewhere back in the Jesus Tomb.

The Annuals

You might not be able to buy them at the Home Depot garden department, but they are annuals nonetheless. These are the people who reliably show their faces in church once or twice a year, usually at Christmas and Easter. Besides elves and bunnies, they are the only creatures who adhere to this schedule. Study their faces well and get their names, because chances are you won't be seeing them back in church for at least another four to seven months.

Annuals always stick out like a sore Hare Krishna, mostly because they never know what to do during a church service. They kneel when they should stand, sit when they should kneel, and can't make heads or tails of the books in the pew. You can always spot them by the intense way they focus on their pew mates in a desperate attempt to ape the actions of the congregation. They stick out as much as Snooki at a debutante ball. I always try to make sudden movements, just to throw them off. Nothing says good will towards men like confusing the annuals on Christmas.

From the way they fight for seats, you would think they were regulars. I remember one Christmas eve walking to the front of the church and spotting some empty space in the pews. I asked a lone woman, whom I didn't recognize, if her empty pew was free. She looked at me like I was wearing a scarlet letter.

She shook her head, "This row and the one behind it are taken."

"Are you new to the parish?" I asked.

"No, we come here every Christmas," she said, adjusting her glasses.

We sat in the pew anyway. Unless you're willing to dedicate yourself week in and week out like the rest of us, and contribute to the church, don't expect reserved premium seating. Had she attended a few more Masses, she would have known that around here, the last shall be first.

Writhing While Tithing

As I was walking into church a few weeks back a family pulled up in a Mercedes station wagon and they piled out of the car in what looked like typical Brooks Brothers fashion. The mom was carrying a venti-something from Starbucks.

The clan took the pew in front of me, and I paid them no further attention—until the collection basket arrived. The father pulled out his billfold and after flipping past several twenties, dropped exactly one dollar into the basket. Let me get this straight. Six dollars for the drink. One dollar for Jesus. I hope their barista will save them a place in Paradise.

These are the same people who you will find after church in the Four Seasons brunch line or dropping hundreds to play a round of golf. Way to store those riches in heaven.

Stand-up Homily

Have you ever been sitting in your pew on Sunday, when all of a sudden your priest or minister hits you with a pop culture reference? They weave them into the sermons in an effort to "connect" with young people and seem "relevant." In the end, it always makes them sound more out of touch and less convincing than had they just stuck to the scripture. Of course, we want these timeless teachings applied to the present day, but it's disconcerting when a religious leader does that by constantly letting us know how "plugged in" he is. He should be focused on the eternal, not into the latest episode of *True Blood*.

Never will I forget the Sunday evening Mass I attended a few years back at a church in downtown D.C. The fifty-something priest started his homily with an attention grabber: "I was watching *American Idol* recently and thought . . ." Everything else he said sounded like static to me. Though typically reserved at mass, I groaned (louder than I should have), "What?!" I looked down the pew and across the aisle. No other parishioner seemed fazed. I suppose it could have been worse; he could have sung from the pulpit like an *Idol* contestant.

Then there are Sundays where you're not quite sure if Father John is in the pulpit, or Ray Romano. These jokesters always have to pepper their homilies with yuks. During Lent, I was traveling and heard a priest open his set this way: "Did you hear the one about the atheist who turned up at the Catholic wake? The atheist came to pay his respects to his friend. When he walked up to the open coffin, the dead guy looked better than he did in life. The atheist leaned in and said, 'Look at you, Arthur, all dressed up and nowhere to go.'" Ba-dump-bump. Father, I expect to hear you talk about the last supper, not appear on Last Comic Standing. I turned to a friend of mine and said, "Is there a cover charge and two-drink minimum for this homily?" The delivery and timing of these jokes are always off, and the message is ultimately diminished. Memo to jokey pastors and priests: once the congregation gets the sin and redemption part down, then you can start doing jokes. Though last time I checked, Jesus didn't sit around the last supper tossing off one-liners.

The Church Clap-Trap

I have nothing against applauding for a soloist belting out a Staple Singers song at a Baptist church in Tennessee, but otherwise it is not a welcome practice in a church setting. I'm talking about people who clap after sermons or other emotional "pitches" for money. It makes worship feel like a performance. And just because one of the schoolkids stood at the mike and awkwardly announced the Girl Scout bake sale, a round of supportive applause is not necessary.

Clapping at church makes about as much sense as clapping at the movies. Unless you're at a premiere, the actors and directors can't hear you! In church, God doesn't need the reinforcement.

He'll be the ultimate judge as to whether something is worthy or not. What's next? Yells of "Bravo" and a standing O after Proverbs 3:6 is read?

Performance Worship

Church should not be a showcase for your song and dance abilities—or lack thereof. I know St. Augustine said "to sing is to pray twice," but he didn't hear what I've been exposed to. Some of the "worship music" that has passed these ears would make the Lord demand extra prayers—of repentance! A congregation raising its voice to God is fine, but outside of a few black churches and the rare traditional choirs, no other singing should be allowed in the sanctuary. Jesus did not play the guitar, the bongos, the bass, the snare drum, or the harmonica. Yet somehow the Almighty has managed to communicate His message of redemption for millennia without the help of a hip-hop beat. Let's keep it that way. I have similarly hostile feelings toward liturgical dancers.

Liturgical dance is for those too uncoordinated or large to dance in any other setting. Until I saw my first liturgical dance, I didn't even know they made leotards in those sizes. These "dance ministers" rely upon our charity, hoping the sacred backdrop will anesthetize us to their lack of talent. A woman in a shroud doing ersatz Martha Graham moves is neither impressive nor inspiring. Why exactly is billowing fabric and spastic movement suddenly sacred? It all looks like charades at Mark Morris's house to me.

Though I must say in fairness, liturgical dance does encourage prayer. The entire congregation is always united, begging God to quickly put an end to the embarrassing display.

Lacking Grace

I understand why so many churchgoers are in need of grace, because an awful lot of them display so very little.

Why, knowing that you are about to shake hands with fellow congregants, either at the start of a service or during the Sign of Peace, would you pick your nose? Do these rude people (who I think have season tickets to the pew in front of mine) imagine that we don't see them sneaking a dig? Confession: I have actually gotten up and taken my children to the back of the church before the Sign of the Peace to avoid shaking hands with the parish pickers.

My friend Ina told me she has seen people at her church's "summer services" surfing the Internet on their iPhones. They put the phones on mute and scroll through their texts and email in the middle of Sunday observances. Just because it's summer, doesn't mean you can "vacation" from decorum in the church! The summer weather seems to bring out the worst in some churchgoers, and it's not just what they are doing, but what they are wearing.

As the temperature rises, beachwear becomes the norm among some congregations. Shorts, sarong-like wraps, swim trunks, and flip-flops (which some wear year-round) are routine. Unless your church is on a sand dune, these fashions are not only unwelcome but scary to many fellow parishioners. It reminds me of the woman I once saw exit a confessional in full body-hugging spandex. I don't know if there was a spin class in there or what—but this was one spiritually dissonant image I could have lived without.

The only thing possibly more obnoxious than the outrageous church fashions is the couples who are forever caressing each other in the pews. I suppose they do it initially to acknowledge a point of mutual interest being made from the pulpit. But there are other cases of roving fingers that I can't explain at all. One man I saw rubbed his wife's back for an entire sermon. I've also seen people stroke their partner's arms, legs, necks, even buttocks during services. Excuse me, but this is supposed to be worship, not a conjugal visit! The only conception I'm even remotely interested in thinking about during church is the immaculate variety.

Pew Buffet

We all struggle to give our full attention to the Gospel reading at church. But last week, the distraction was so powerful my attention wandered. A chomping sound was coming from the pew in front of me. It reverberated on the wood, creating the audio equivalent of pigs at a trough. Leaning forward, I spied two children, between their parents, sitting on the kneeler, eating off the pew. Scattered across the varnished wood were Goldfish, Cheerios, peanuts, sippy cups, and enough race cars to have a miniature Talladega Speedway run. Isn't it wonderful to see families so comfortable in church that they feel free to drag the contents of their snack cabinet and half the kids' toy collection with them? It's sort of their own portable rec room. At Christmas, I look forward to seeing them fill the pew with Ping-Pong tables and wide-screen TVs.

Just as I am trying to teach my kids reverence for the liturgy and the importance of being quiet, these people decide to hold a snacking and playtime demonstration. Your roving picnic is disturbing children and adults alike. We're not amused by your son's ability to hurl Cheetos across the floor, and the Noah's Ark coloring books do nothing to compensate for his failure to pay attention. I have to say I was proud when my little son, with a furrowed brow, scanned the junk food banquet littering the pew in front of him and announced, "Big mess." I'll say. Unless your kid is going to multiply the Goldfish to feed 5,000, keep them in the pantry and out of the pews.

Tithe-a-vangelists

Their most devoted viewers are probably insomniacs. After tossing and turning, you flip on the TV at 3 a.m. and are sure to find a perfectly tailored man or woman striding across a stage holding "church." New televangelists pop up every week. With their *Battlestar Galactica* couture and Day-Glo dye jobs, they have carved out a unique place in the media landscape. And don't you just love the middle-aged guys in the designer T-shirts and sneakers preaching to the "youth"? Dressing like a kid does not make them more receptive to you. If you think I'm wrong, try evangelizing the toddlers while donning a romper.

The theology of the televangelist crowd is universally light, but the moment tithing comes up, they all turn into Thomas Aquinas. Suddenly the early church fathers, ancient texts, and tales of the miraculous are invoked to convince the viewer that "a love offering" is the only way to release the "blessing that God has in store for you." One televangelist is appropriately named Creflo Dollar, pastor of the World Changers Church in Georgia. He became a YouTube sensation after sharing his personal fantasy. In the daydream, any of his congregants who failed to tithe would be lined up and the ushers would "shoot 'em all dead." I must have missed that moment in the scripture when the Lord turns to his disciples and says: "Let the little children come to me and do not hinder them. Those offering tithes are a part of me. Pray that the others are wearing flak jackets."

Televangelists come in two varieties: "the Arena Headliner"

or "the Public Access Small-Timer." The Arena Headliner is
the star of his or her own stadium event. Tens of thousands of
people are in attendance, the lighting is dramatic, the choir is
magnificent—the only thing you won't see is an image of Jesus
or a cross. Arena Headliners have a standard opener with a trite
anecdote or a joke that seems cribbed from an old *Reader's Digest.* I recently experienced this piece of deep theology: "My wife
and I love to bake, and we use that stuff called Pam—so things
don't stick to the cookie sheet. And you know, faith in Jesus is
like Pam. With faith nothing sticks to you." Thanks, C. S. Lewis.

The Public Access Small-Timer has not been quite so
successful—or has fallen on hard times. Though he remains on
television, the Small Timer's congregation is severely diminished,
and it shows. Whereas the big guys broadcast from sports arenas,
these folks preach from tiny sets with styrofoam back drops. In
the middle of their sermonizing, the video will abruptly cut to
canned footage to hide the fact that their flock abandoned them
years ago. When the women laughing at the jokes are wearing
beehives and cat eyeglasses, you know this is not a contemporary
crowd. The only ones listening now are a half-sleeping camera-
man, an arthritic basset hound, and the operator in the next
room manning the donation lines.

A Mormon by Any Other Name

Why is it that Mormons now get upset when you call them
Mormons? They now prefer to be called Latter-day Saints. As

the old saying goes, "I have a lot of friends who are Mormons" who give me dirty looks each time I say "Mormon"—which is saying something. Have you ever tried to upset a Mormon—uh, Latter-day Saint? It takes a lot. They're very nice people.

The term "Mormon" is derived from the Book of Mormon, which Mormons—I mean, Latter-day Saints—revere. The more I thought about it, the more it made sense. Imagine if people started calling Christians "Biblers" or referring to Muslims as "Korans." Still, "Latter-day Saint" doesn't exactly trip off the tongue. Maybe we can compromise and just call them "Latters."

Whatever you call the Mormons, all I know is, my kids think they have the coolest architecture outside the Vatican. And I can't wait to show them the golden plates. Where are those things kept now, anyway?

People of the Book

Peace be upon the Muslims (and upon non-Muslims as well). As Barack Obama never tires of reminding us, Muslims have contributed so much to our culture: the development of algebra, elegant architecture, and the world's most effective means of spreading athlete's foot. The Muslims I know are wonderful people devoted to family and community. Two Muslim friends of mine are among the best doctors in D.C., both of whom are outraged by the radical elements in Islam, particularly their treatment of women.

Women have it rough in Islam. Unless head coverings are your thing and your color wheel is black—your fashion choices are limited. During a recent trip to Disney World, I found myself standing behind a woman in a full burka at Epcot. I thought I was looking at the Experimental Prototype Community of Tomorrow. From my vantage point, it looked more like the twelfth century. Ninety-six degrees out and the woman is boarding Test Track dressed like Harry Potter's worst nightmare. I wanted to give the poor dear a fan. As I watched her, I thought, "She has to be hotter than the guy in the Mickey Mouse costume. And no one is even asking to take his picture with her."

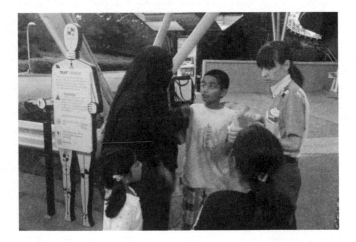

I have run across observant Muslim women at the gym, as well. Here I am in my workout shorts and a T-shirt when this woman steps onto an adjacent treadmill wearing a raincoat and a hijab. She worked out for the next hour. She wore the raincoat the entire time. The husband showed up a bit later wearing a muscle shirt and basketball shorts. But at least the woman was allowed to go to the gym. At the mosque she would be left at the door, somewhere near the pile of shoes.

Incidentally, does anybody know when we changed the nomenclature from Moslem to Muslim? Probably at the same time we went from Mormons to Latter-day Saints.

Father Sally

Call me anti-woman if you must—but do you get skeptical at a funeral service when a woman comes out in a Roman collar and a chasuble to offer prayers for the deceased? A funeral is depressing enough without having to sit through a message by a nondenominational female cleric wearing a multi-hued woven frock.

Father Sally's homily usually comes off sounding like Eckhart Tolle at an Earth Day rally. We don't show up at church to listen to your political speeches or Earth Mother sermons. Stick to redemption, sister.

I've heard all the arguments on both sides of the ordained women debate: there were women who served the early Christian community, women were the first ones to discover the resurrection ... Here's what we know: Jesus chose twelve guys to follow Him and perpetuate His church. He vested the twelve with authority and commanded them to spread His message and His sacraments. They were all men. Of course I'm not saying women can't serve the church in critical ways—but is service only possible via cross-dressing? There is no disputing the fact that women were among Jesus's disciples, and that they made contributions to the early church. But you'll notice the scripture says nothing about an alternative group of gal pals hanging with Jesus on the weekends. Women were never ordained in the early church, and contrary to the opinion of some, the Lord and His Apostles were not the original inspiration for *Charlie's Angels*.

Door-to-Door Snore

I am in the middle of dinner and the doorbell rings. There on my front stoop are two young women wearing the sickly sweet smiles of people who have had the door slammed in their faces one too many times. They look as if they would continue smiling even if a brick were thrown at their heads. The Jehovah's Witnesses have returned at the most inappropriate time.

"We want to invite you to a special biblical talk."

"Oh really," I say, wiping my mouth. "What kind of biblical talk?"

"It's all about how you can apply biblical principles to your life." They thrust a pamphlet and a magazine into my hand. Though I explain that I am a Catholic and in the middle of a meal, they continue their patter. "The teachings of the Bible can turn your life around," one of them says. (Not exactly a great argument, since their Bible obviously has no prohibition on interrupting people during dinner.)

Hastily closing the door, I study the pamphlet in my hand. It's a pastel-colored invite, obviously modeled on an Easter card. This is odd since Jehovah's Witnesses don't celebrate Easter—they consider it pagan. Yet there on the back of the thing is Jesus seated on a stone surrounded by flowers—though to my Catholic eyes, he looks more like St. Jude having a sit in the back garden. Both the invite and the *Watchtower* are promptly deposited in the recycle bin.

A bit of advice to my Jehovah's Witness friends: the mail is the most efficient way to convey your written materials to strangers. And if you truly want to win converts to your faith, you may want to confine your pitch to non-dining hours.

Interreligious Dialogue

Meaningless. You believe one thing, we believe another.

Acknowledgments

My children inspired me to make this comedic turn away from politics and toward the culture. During the mad sprint to complete this work, Maria and Dmitri kept me laughing, and reminded me each day why it all matters. They are blessed to have their Arroyo brothers and sisters: Alexander, Lorenzo, and Mariella. Rebecca Arroyo held it together with her customary grace and ample doses of her spunky, positive spirit. Chris Edwards was a rock who provided invaluable guidance, support, and some great photos. Sahaira and Carly were indispensable team players. My producers—Matt, Max, and Alyssa—kept the show going strong when I was juggling everything else. Bill O'Reilly, Bill Shine, John Ferriter, Don Imus, Bernard McGuirk, Eric Weissler, Rick Bernthal, and the great Roger Ailes continue to be trusted supporters and friends. My thanks to you all.

Threshold Editions' Louise Burke, Anthony Ziccardi, Jeremie Ruby-Strauss, Emilia Pisani, and Jennifer Robinson have all shepherded this work from concept to bookshelves in splendid fashion. A special shout-out to Michael Nagin, who designed this eye-popping cover, and to Deborah Feingold, who braved the Delaware River to snap the golden shot.

A special thanks to Julie Altman and Sue Reichel for their input and sharp-eyed edits and to Tim and Kate O'Neill, my Russia support system. As always, thanks to Stephen Vaughn for his adroit counsel and steadfast support. Affection and thanks to the Cipollones, who always have an open door. And to the Longs and Collotons for friendship and laughs for twenty-five years. I owe so much to Chuck and Ina Carlsen, my Washington parents and fun grandparents. We love you. My brothers across the miles—Curtis and Brooks, Jim and Stephanie; my father, Jim Ingraham, and the memory of my mother are always in my heart. As for Raymond Arroyo—his talent and wit are amazing, but his strength, loyalty, and faith are what make him great. And finally, I am grateful above all for God's abundant blessings.